NAKED
AND NOT
ASHAMED

NAKED
AND NOT
ASHAMED

DAN SCOTT

HARVEST HOUSE PUBLISHERS

EUGENE, OREGON

Cover by Left Coast Design, Portland, Oregon

Cover photo © Jennie Warren / Corbis

Back cover author photo by Danile Bell

Dan Scott: Published in association with Borquez-Guess Literary Agency, 168 Cavalcade Circle, Franklin, TN 37069.

Unless otherwise noted, the stories in this book are fictitious accounts, used for illustration purposes only. Although based on the author's experiences, they are not meant to refer to any person, living or dead.

Library of Congress Cataloging-in-Publication Data
Scott, Dan, 1953-
Naked and not ashamed / Dan Scott.
  p. cm.
ISBN-13: 978-0-7369-2190-9
ISBN-10: 0-7369-2190-7
1. Sex—Religious aspects—Christianity. I. Title.
BT708.S37 2008
233.'5—dc22

                                                        2007019414

To Trish, my wife

And to all the people
who helped us heal

Acknowledgments

I would like to thank Terry Glaspey and Gene Skinner for being good writing coaches and editors. My daughter Tiffany Cagle did a lot of the early editing on the emerging manuscript. Michelle Borquez believed in the manuscript and took it to Harvest House. Lisa Hennis' extensive commentary on my manuscript helped me enormously as I worked on the final draft. My daughter Talitha Kartler put up with many conversations about the book and made suggestions about how to make it relevant to her generation and to women. And my sons-in-law were patient with me as I hijacked so much of their wives' time while I was working on the book.

CONTENTS

Introduction

Sex is a hot subject. A trained professor can sometimes manage to make sex boring, but that usually takes years of education. Otherwise, the mere mention of sex normally captures our attention. I'm not sure why; perhaps sex reminds us that we're alive. As Walter Percy once said, "Dead men don't get erections!"

I wouldn't put it that crudely. It's really not about erections; it's about an intimate connection with another person's body and heart. It's about seeing our soul reflected in his or her eyes.

Our need to experience this life-affirming connection is the heart of sexual attraction. It is also the fuel of sexual addiction.

In our present culture, which has closed so many of its spiritual doors, men and women cling to this one remaining pathway to meaning and transcendence. This sets the stage for a continual conflict between religious moralists and sexual libertines. Without some sense of the infinite, people who want to know they are more than machines have few options in a secular age like ours. A religious person can cling to what he believes to be the law of God regardless of whether he actually has a sense of His presence. A truly secular person, however, cannot hold to a moral code based on a religious system. The middle ground between secular and religious people has thus become difficult to find because their frames of reference are now so different.

Our culture, on both the right and the left, increasingly experiences itself as godless. The left tends to fill the spiritual vacuum with orgiastic ideas—oneness with the earth, solidarity with the masses, faith in cosmic evolution, and so forth. The right fills the vacuum with law and wealth, believing that if we can only stabilize society, individual initiative will find its way and lead us all out of darkness. Nonetheless, when the office closes and the solitary night settles in, people on both the right and the left want to touch something beyond biology and economics. They want to experience themselves as alive and meaningful to the universe. That's when the urge for sexual connection—even a make-believe one on the Internet—can become so compelling to so many.

So I wanted to write a book about the Christian meaning of sex and to explain to my fellow believers why sexuality has become so important to our secular neighbors. I also wanted to explain to non-Christians why we believe our culture's drift toward sexual anarchy threatens the foundations of civilized life.

For many, sex has become the only way to awaken the spirit. When we have sex, we at least know we have a soul; we remember that we are more than wage earners. So sex has become for many a place to recover one's being. Besides, as the historic churches have gradually succumbed to the same loss of soul as the culture at large, sex as a meaning-bestowing experience has become as important to Christians as to non-Christians. When people have no opportunity for transcendence through worship, sex often becomes an important sacrament and sanctuary, even for believers.

Christians used to take for granted that worship was mostly about connecting their souls to God. They went to church to "taste of the powers of the world to come."[1] Now, even for conservative American believers, worship is usually more about community with other people than about experiencing the presence of God. At best, we go to church now to learn about God—we do not expect Him to overwhelm us until heaven becomes more real to us than earth.

However, that's what transcendence is: becoming aware of the beyond, remembering that this is not all there is. Worship was supposed to be the place where that happened. If it is not, then what is?

Well, for many people, sex is.

If this has become true for many Christians, we can understand why our secular friends have become so defensive when believers suggest that sex ought to be restrained or controlled in any way. Our faith requires us to set boundaries and limits around our sexual lives. However, people in our culture now view such teachings as antiquated and even pathological; they sincerely believe we are trying to rob them of one of life's greatest joys.

For much of our society, sex has become precious as well as fun; it is as much a religion as a form of recreation. Like all things precious, sex now sparks the most intense debates and unleashes divisive passions. Even Christian churches have been reeling from parishioners' polarizing attitudes and beliefs about sexuality. So we cannot label the different opinions about sex as "Christian" and "non-Christian." Many Christians no longer share an understanding about sexual matters.

A popular show at the time of this writing, *Studio 60 on the Sunset Strip,* has a character named Harriett Hays. Although a single Christian, she does not live a celibate life. In her words, "If I weren't having premarital sex, I'd probably die a virgin."

In fact, many Christians now deny there *is* such a thing as a Christian view of sexuality. Of course, this is a recent opinion. Until the last few years, all Christians shared a basic understanding that Christian sexuality was necessarily heterosexual and covenantal. However, that is no longer the case.

Christians, like their secular neighbors, are confused and conflicted over sexual issues. So if we intend to make a case for biblical morality—even to our Christian children and grandchildren, not to speak of making the case to our secular culture—we must honestly recognize this. We can have all the "covenant ring" ceremonies we want, but many Christian young people are not grasping why sex is such a big deal. Like the culture at large, they need to know that sex is good but that it needs boundaries to remain good. They also need to know that sex is not God.

You may have already decided that this book is about recovering past beliefs about morality. If so, you are only partly right. The sexual revolution has been a disaster; it was also unavoidable. For centuries, Christians embraced a sexual theology that caused much pain. It cursed what our own Scriptures blessed and gave us a faith that was cognitively impressive but emotionally impoverished. Our gonads could not accept the tyranny of this disembodied spirituality. They sizzled in silence while our preachers denounced them and our sexuality gathered its force for the explosion to come.

Then the explosion came.

In the sexual revolution, baby boomers tore down our culture's sexual restraints. Most of our contemporaries hail this as one of the great accomplishments of the twentieth century, though not everyone agrees, including Peter Kreeft, a highly respected author and Roman Catholic ethicist.

> The sexual revolution will quite possibly prove to be the most destructive in history, far more than any political or military revolution, because it touches not only lives, but the very wellspring of life.[2]

What a phrase—"the wellspring of life"! It reveals why sex is so intimately connected to our spirituality and why it impacts us as it does. For sex does indeed touch the wellspring of life in more ways than the obvious. Of course it involves the wellspring of biological life. However, sex is also the wellspring of our social life and spiritual lives.

Parents who lack sexual harmony struggle to develop happy and emotionally stable families. Without stable families, community is difficult to create. Thus, healthy sex nourishes community, and unhealthy sex consumes it. The story of Sodom powerfully illustrates this principle.

In Sodom, as the book of Genesis tells the story, men were inflamed with unbridled sexual desire that reduced individuals to mere orifices. If a grown man were not available, perhaps a young girl would do; if not a man or a girl, perhaps even an angel. Nothing was sexually off-limits in Sodom. Finally, even the city's one righteous man was drugged and seduced by his own daughters.

What began as a sexual heat ended in a fiery conflagration that destroyed everything. As Leon Kass remarked, "This is not only what happened; it is what always happens."

For a Christian, healthy sex is about boundaries as well as freedom.

Deciding what (or who) defines sex as healthy or unhealthy quickly propels us toward either the political right or the left, toward the red or the blue. Then, once we have taken our side in the current cultural conflict, we may no longer feel compelled to explain our choices to those on the other side.

However, failing to explain ourselves makes our moral opinions feel groundless to our children and to the culture at large. Few people are willing to say no to sex just because we say they should. If we make moral demands "just because our religion says so," modern people simply walk away from religion.

So how do we talk about sex to modern people in a way that is both relevant and faithful to Scripture?

For starters, most of us will agree that sex, like spirituality, gets lost in abstraction and theory. Like spirituality, sex is a contact sport, a relationship more than a philosophy. So our culture deserves more than a detached conversation about moral rectitude. A theology of sex has to recognize that we are sexual beings because God made us that way. It has to teach us that God delights in our expression of erotic life within the boundaries He has fixed. It also has to be honest about the fact that most of us want sex.

We must also recognize that our culture had a sexual revolution because people wanted more than morality; they wanted to be touched. They wanted to experience guiltless passion with their beloved. Most of us, even many in the far right, deeply sympathize with those aims, however we vote and however we pray. So we don't want to turn the clock back.

However, that doesn't mean the past has nothing to say to us.

Our ancestors had spiritual understanding that helped them preserve their families and civilization despite their often unfulfilled hopes for sexual intimacy. No doubt their sexual struggle was a private pain that many of them had to stoically accept. We can only shake our heads at the sorrow this caused them. On the other hand, the sexual revolution has not proven to be much of a cure. Our search for true intimacy has proven as elusive since the '60s as before, and we are arguably less spiritually fulfilled than our ancestors.

The sexual revolution (like most revolutions) set up a greater tyranny than the one it overthrew. By destroying the boundaries of traditional morality, the sexual revolution seriously damaged the foundation on which family, nation, church, and individual happiness rests. It challenged not only Christian morality but also the morality upheld by civilizations and religions of nearly every age. This has left many of us empty and longing for something that will touch our souls.

This is not to agree with those who demonize sexuality, who want us to pretend we never passed through puberty. We don't stop wanting sex just because we are born-again. Christians have genitals. Besides, like the rest of humanity, we are fallen creatures, and our sexual desires are not always compatible with our faith. So Christians would be dishonest to claim that our moral beliefs somehow protect us from sexual struggle. Most believers have profited from the sexual revolution as well as struggled with it. Christians should acknowledge these things before trying to critique our culture's morals.

At the same time, we must examine the damage the sexual revolution has caused. For example, our new myths promise that in a "healthy relationship"—our modern culture would never say marriage—sex is always earth-shattering; lightning strikes, firecrackers explode, and people forget their names. This sexual perfectionism is every bit as tyrannical as the Puritanism we claim to have outgrown. Our attempts to make the exceptional experience into the norm inevitably set us up for frustration and addiction. As a result, our sexual pain may be greater than that of our ancestors, despite our new freedoms.

Naturally, we want sex to be powerful and fulfilling. However, life can be cruel. Bad childhood experiences, molestation, shame, silence, inappropriate kinds of early exposure to sex—all of these things work havoc on a developing sexuality. Many people arrive at adulthood sexually challenged. They sometimes have to work long and hard to undo the damage. Besides, even good sex is not God.

Sex is a part of nature. We can know nature, even intimately, without coming to know God.

To meet God, we need transcendent worship, worship that helps us connect our soul to the presence of God. We also need a covenant with the Almighty and His people that provides the structure within which transcendent experience takes place and gradually shapes us into new people.

Sex can't do all of that.

Deifying sex has caused much suffering in modern culture, especially for the children and spouses whose parents and partners abandoned them because they wanted better sex. Although the breakup of the family has many causes (including economic ones), the sexual revolution's attempt to replace spiritual life must own up to its share of the blame.

Thus, neither the moralizing of the religious right nor the sexual libertarianism of the secular left has enough depth to answer the sexual issues of modern life. Even if we wanted to, we can't return to our grandparents' universe, as some would have us do. However, neither should we surrender to an immoral culture, where covenants are broken and children are marginalized.

So Christians need a theology of sex, one that assumes that God has the right to order our lives so we may "glorify God and enjoy Him forever."[3] Many of us struggle to enjoy Him because our sexual lives have been disordered and painful, so spiritual growth must necessarily involve understanding what it means to be a sexual being.

So this is a book about sex. It is also about facing the implications of serving One who created us to be sexual beings. In it, I will claim that what touches our bodies affects our souls and that our souls express themselves through our bodies. I will argue that far from being a distraction from spiritual life, sex is a form of spiritual life. Therefore, sex deserves a respect that is not idolatrous and requires restraints that are not oppressive.

To the extent that it is possible to do so in a fallen and imperfect world, we want to learn how to be like Adam and Eve when their love was yet innocent and whole. We want to be naked and not ashamed.

Epiphany, 2007
Nashville, Tennessee

One

A Big Fat Jewish Wedding

I always thought it something of a mystery—even an embarrassment—that Jesus began His ministry with such a trivial and irresponsible miracle.

Without a doubt, turning water into wine is impressive. Surely, though, the Lord Jesus Christ could have found a more worthy manner in which to begin His mission to a needy world! He could have healed someone, for example. He could have revealed some mystery of faith that would have astounded the people of ancient Palestine. He could have removed the thorns from the roses as a down payment of the earth's coming redemption.

He did none of this. Instead, He turned water into wine. Good wine to be sure; wine so impressive the host claimed it to be the best he had ever tasted. But wine nonetheless.

Why?

I never understood why Jesus performed this miracle until I saw *My Big Fat Greek Wedding*. That's when it hit me; Middle Easterners didn't have 30-minute weddings. They had three-day weddings! Weddings were about more than just a couple getting married; they were about renewing the relationships within an entire community.

As Jesus began His ministry, He wanted to make a statement about life. Two young people had just been married. They could hardly go away to the Hilton or the Holiday Inn. Somehow, they had to find privacy in their little town, in a hut with one or two rooms. This might be the only time in their lives when they would have real privacy, so they needed a good party to keep everyone away. They needed space so they could giggle and moan, so they could abandon themselves to each other in these first hours of their shared lives.

That's why the party needed wine.

Normally, Jewish people didn't drink much. Since most fortified spirits wouldn't come along until late medieval times, if people wanted to get drunk, they had to work at it. (The Chinese had already learned how to make liquor by the time of Christ, but the peoples of the Middle East would not learn how to fortify naturally fermented juice until AD 800.) Drunkards weren't well thought of in the ancient world. However, if someone did happen to drink too much at an event like a wedding, the worst thing likely to happen was that he would stumble as he walked home. No one would be in any great danger from his overindulgence—he wouldn't be driving a car! He would sleep it off and then prepare himself for his neighbors' inevitable teasing.

People's lives were brutal and brief. A special feast, like a wedding, was a great treat. It gave townspeople a chance to play games, tell stories, and enjoy one another. It not only marked a personal rite of passage for a new couple but also helped preserve their community.

Jesus knew all of this when He attended that wedding. He knew that after the wedding, a young man and young woman would be learning how to be intimate with each other inside a crude little hut. He knew they were counting on the party to keep people away during their special time together. He also knew the townspeople were looking forward to the festival because they needed a break from their hard work.

So the occasion was a sacred one—a holy celebration of covenant. However, it was also a fun break from everyday life. That's how holy days become holidays, but Jesus despised neither. He knew that each supported the other.

Jesus also knew that He had come to bring life. Unlike the Pharisees, He didn't offer legalism as a way to God. He wasn't trying to find life by becoming a hermit, a vegetarian, or an anorexic. Jesus loved life too much to deny it. The time would come when He would have to suffer and die, but not today. Today, His message was about life and joy.

These must have been some of the Master's thoughts as He responded to His mother's words, "They have no wine."

That's why, unlike me, Jesus didn't look at this miracle as a trivial use of His power. He intentionally chose this moment to make a statement about what He valued: community, marriage, joy, intimacy, and yes, sex.

THOSE NASTY GNOSTICS

My interpretation of the Lord's first miracle upsets some people. I think I know why!

Early in Christian history, some believers began trying to become spiritual by disconnecting from their bodily needs. In time, this search came to be known as Gnosticism. Although the Christian church officially denounced it, many Gnostic teachings lodged, like a virus, into the popular beliefs of Christian people. So the Gnostic virus has deeply affected Christians' attitudes about life in general but especially about sexuality. As a result, Christians have often heard subliminal messages that poison our sexuality. Consider some of the contradictory messages young Christians often hear about sex:

- If you save yourself for that special one, God will give you mind-blowing sex on your honeymoon. (In some Christian groups, waiting may mean no dating, holding hands, or kissing.)

- You won't need any special instruction or preparation; it just happens as an act of divine grace.

- Once you are married, sex will be a sacred duty whether you like it or not.

- The holier you become, the less you will want sex. When you become really spiritual, you probably won't want it at all.

- You shouldn't abandon yourself to "bestial" urges (moaning, groaning, and the like). Control yourself.

- Sexual matters will work themselves out. You don't need a sexual education. God will be angry if you look at any sexual material, whatever your intent.

- As you become increasingly holy, you will return to your prepubescent state of childlike innocence.

- Be careful to not deviate much from straightforward sexual intercourse.

Many Christians will recognize messages like these. Though rarely stated outright, they are implied in conversations about sex with Sunday school teachers, parents, and other authority figures. Although some people promote these teachings as a path to moral purity, they are "crazy making" because they drive believers into a "damned if you do, damned if you don't" cul-de-sac. They also demonize the body and its appetites, which God Himself created and called good.

The messages imply something like this: God wants to give us a special gift that we must not open until the right time. It is so powerful and wonderful that it will drastically change our lives, and we will know how to enjoy it without any special instruction. However, as we become spiritual, we probably won't want it. Then, if we learn not to want this gift, God will reward us by sending us to a special place where it doesn't exist!

No wonder our sexuality can take such strange and pathological paths!

Harmful messages like these can keep us from accepting ourselves as sexual beings. They don't do a good job of stopping us from wanting sex though. We get caught in a constant tug-of-war between desire and avoidance that becomes a tormenting stress for those who want to live holy lives.

CUTTING THE GNOSTIC KNOT

When Alexander the Great reached the border of Persia, he saw a knotted rope. An ancient prophecy claimed the East could only be conquered by the man who untied this "Gordian knot." As his advisers gathered around to see what the great general would do, they were amazed to see him take out his sword and simply sever the knot!

That guy didn't fool around with foolish complexities!

Sometimes things get too complicated to unravel piece by piece. Gnosticism is one of them. It looks formidable, it ties us in knots, and it's contrary to the gospel. If we want to have good sex, or a healthy spiritual life, we have to cut the Gnostic knot!

Gnosticism is profoundly wrong in its contempt for the body. Souls do not become purified and prepared to abandon their earthly prison. Souls need bodies in order to communicate with other souls. If we try to become disembodied, we don't become holy; we become isolated and weird.

That's not holiness; it's masochism. It's also nuts!

Jesus turned water into wine so the party could go on, so the couple in the hut could find ecstasy and delight in each other's arms. His words "I have come that they may have life, and have it to the full" were not mere theological abstractions. They were also not just about heaven. Jesus wanted everyone to have a good time. There would be a day for dying and a time to sweat great drops of blood. But not today. Today was a time to laugh. Today was a time to make love. So Jesus told the servants, "Fill the waterpots with water!"

SACRED SEXUALITY

So how does a Christian begin to accept sexuality as a gift from God? How do we learn to receive and give sexual pleasure without guilt?

If we believe in the incarnation, the resurrection of the body, and the creation (including sex) as God's handiwork, sex should be a joyful and fulfilling experience. However, the Bible does not offer much practical advice on sexual matters other than warning us about what to avoid. Only one book in the Bible deals specifically with erotic love: Song of Solomon (or the Song of Songs, as our Jewish and Catholic friends prefer to call it).

However, before we look at this part of our own sacred text, let's take a look at how people in other religions have dealt with the connection between the erotic and the spiritual. Sometimes when we hear how other cultures experience life, familiar things can become fresh again. That happened to me after I read the Kama Sutra. Afterward, when I reread the Song of Solomon, the erotic nature of our own Scripture became much clearer.

A BOOK OF LOVE

Westerners usually use the Kama Sutra as a pretext for soft pornography. For Hindus, however, it is a serious exploration of erotic love and of the way sexual intimacy can lead to spiritual life. A teacher named Vatsyayana wrote the Kama Sutra ("Rules of Love") in the fourth century AD, and it quickly took its place within a body of Hindu literature called "kalas" (or "arts").

The kalas explore the implications of Hindu spirituality for various disciplines and activities of life. For example, they reflect on the spiritual implications of eating. Indian cuisine thus encourages one to educate his or her palate by deliberately expanding his or her culinary taste. It also encourages chefs to use spice, color, and texture to promote community among people and between people and God. Toward that end, a cook should conduct a "symphony of taste" with cayenne pepper, yogurt, sweet and sour fruits and vegetables, bitter and bland sauces, rough and smooth seeds, and nuts. The result of this culinary diversity is a meal that stimulates as many of the senses as possible, so those who eat the meal will linger to savor it. As they do, they deepen their connections with their family and friends. Thus, a well-prepared meal honors God, blesses people, and draws both into community with one another.

The Kama Sutra applies this same idea to lovemaking. It encourages us to expand our capacity for intimate, erotic experience. The Kama Sutra discourages casual sex, even for married people. It suggests that couples should plan specific times when they can create the sorts of sexual experiences that require leisure, learning, and intentional focus.

Some of the techniques described in the Kama Sutra seem contrived, not to mention physically impossible. (At my age, I'm afraid some of those positions would not only fail to bring me ecstatic bliss but also lead to an extended hospital stay!) However, the book does offer some sound practical advice for heightening sexual pleasure. For example, it advises us to breathe through the mouth instead of through the nose as sexual pleasure builds and to vocalize the breathing to make it audible. Then, as orgasm approaches, it advises us to hold our breath.

The Kama Sutra talks a lot about preparation too. It mentions the usefulness of physical exercises to intensify sexual sensation, such as tensing the pelvic floor in a rhythmic way. (We now refer to this as a "Kegel" exercise.) However, most of the preparation is about presentation, about making ourselves and the lovemaking environment ready for a season of erotic pleasure.

Although people often discover physical techniques like these on their own, many do not. At any rate, something is to be said for a religious text that honors and sanctifies the experience of lovemaking, which in turn encourages us to develop our capacity to experience erotic intimacy.

Tantric Buddhism, popular with many rocks stars, including Sting, offers another spiritual approach to sex. It is growing in popularity as a path to spiritual enlightenment through erotic experience. Tantra focuses on cultivating the sensual awareness of one's own body and on understanding the erotic body language of one's lover.

In the end though, an orthodox Christian cannot endorse either the Kama Sutra or Tantric practice. They tempt us to do what St. Paul warns us against in the first chapter of his epistle to the Romans: worshipping the creature rather than the Creator. We cannot cure our culture's historic tendency to suppress sex by turning eroticism into an idol.

The ancient Hebrews spent centuries struggling against Canaanite fertility cults. Biblical spirituality emerged as a response to this struggle and rebukes our natural tendency to treat sex as a path to God. St. Paul draws the same line in Romans 1. Because humanity worshipped the creation rather than the Creator,

> God gave them up to vile passions. For even their women exchanged the natural use for what is against nature. Likewise also the men, leaving the natural use of the woman, burned in their lust for one another, men with men committing what is shameful.

With this caution in mind, we return to our own sacred text to inquire what the Bible teaches us about erotic life. We find there an uninhibited and artful praise of romance and eroticism that honors the spiritual boundaries of our own faith.

Solomon doesn't offer us sexual technique, but his erotic poem does honor sexuality. That's why preachers through the ages have been quick to label the book's eroticism as a metaphor of spiritual life ("the union betwixt Christ and His Church," to quote the old English marriage ceremony). And, metaphor it may be. However, before we can legitimately use the book's sexual language as metaphor, we should first read it for what it clearly is: an erotic story about a prince and a young shepherd woman.[1]

Using the erotic imagery of the Song of Solomon as metaphor is easy because of the intimate connection between sex and spiritual life. However, many preachers have treated the poem's erotic scenes as metaphors because they were uncomfortable with the idea that such blatant eroticism would be included in the holy Word of God. They made it to be about Christ and His church. Nonetheless, reading the poem as allegory does offer valuable insight into the nature of spiritual experience. Indeed, the connection between sex and spiritual life is this book's core idea.

SOLOMON AND THE SHULAMITE

The Song of Songs, like the book of Esther, does not directly mention God. However, as in Esther, His presence permeates the story. The poem's spiritual quality motivated earlier generations to insist that its intent was allegorical. If the apparently erotic elements were meant only to point the soul toward God, then treating this book as Holy Scripture was not so troubling.

As an aside though, erotic elements are also central to the book of Esther. The heroine of that book, like the Shulamite in the Song of Solomon, is noted for her overt sensuality and wins the heart of a king by performing an erotic dance.

The writer of the Song of Solomon (probably the Shulamite) begins by dedicating her story to Solomon, the great and powerful king. It then immediately begins with the explosive demand:

> Kiss me!
> Make me drunk with your kisses.
> For your sweet loving is better than wine.[2]

The speaker is a young peasant Shulamite (woman of Jerusalem) who is experiencing a sexual awakening. She has been smitten by a young man whom she constantly compares to Solomon. She sees him as graceful, dignified, and sexually desirable, and she doesn't mind letting him know how she feels.

She also realizes that he finds her arousing. "I awakened you," she reminds him (8:5). However, she wants him to get on with it. "Let my beloved come into his garden," she says. "There I will give you my love" (4:16; 7:12).

Nearly every layer of the poem is infused with double and triple meanings. It describes the human body as a landscape and the Judean landscape as a human body. It depicts the lovers as animals. It also uses eating and drinking as metaphors for lovemaking. It weaves touch, taste, and scent into a feast for the senses and creates an erotic environment in which the lovers can play their parts.

The Hebrew word in the Song of Solomon that translators usually render as "love" is *dodim*. This word however is closer in meaning to the English street term "lovin'." Thus, we might translate 1:2 this way: "Your sweet lovin' is better than wine." On the other hand, the poem is never coarse. When the Shulamite refers to her sexuality, she always does so in metaphor, thereby guarding her dignity as one made in the image and likeness of God. Her "garden" is fragrant and, in the presence of her lover, is covered with "dew." "Breathe on my garden," she says. "Let its spices stream out. Let my lover come into the garden and taste its delicious fruit."

Her need for him becomes so strong that she almost feels sick. She struggles to know how to contain her aroused emotions and body. When she is in his arms, she says, "His right hand embraces me." However, she knows not to "awaken love until it pleases." She knows how to wait.

Her lover similarly describes their erotic moments in respectful ways. When he remembers their first sexual meeting, he boasts, "I have come into my garden, my sister, my bride." (Until then it had been "her" garden.) "I have gathered my myrrh and my spices. I have eaten from the honeycomb. I have drunk the milk and the wine" (5:1).

As in any good love story, the lovers have to overcome obstacles. The Shulamite's brothers (like most brothers) do not seem to realize that she is no longer a little girl. "Our little sister has no breasts," they say to themselves. "Soon she will come of age, and we need to know how to handle her suitors" (8:8). Meanwhile, she and her lover talk constantly about her breasts. Her lover describes them as towers to climb, grapes to eat, and twin gazelles running through the woods. She also tells how her lover slept through the night with his head between her breasts. All of this is lost on the brothers, who keep talking about their responsibility to protect their innocent little sister. So they keep plotting about how to "catch the little foxes who want to raid our vineyard now that its vines are in blossom" (2:15).

Like all great lovers, this couple finds ways to elude the obstacles and find moments of delight in one another. They make love outdoors where, the Shulamite believes, her lover was conceived. They also make love in a room she has prepared with spices and oils. They romp and rejoice verse after verse, aroused by anticipation, by consummation, and by remembrance of their nights of love.

As we read through this fiery erotic story, we wonder how anyone could have ever missed the point! The lovers tell us in a hundred different ways that they are burning for one another. They discover dozens of ways to make love. They disclose the most intimate details of their encounters, including the taste and fragrance of their bodies.

The poem is sensuous and bold. It is also sacred Scripture.

Eros may be, as many of the church fathers insisted, a lower form of love than agape. However, just as adding and subtracting must precede geometry and calculus, Scripture does not try to teach us about agape until we have learned something about eros. One cannot use something considered profane and base as a metaphor of something that is holy. If we are to read the Song of Solomon as being about Christ and His church or about the soul hungering for the divine, we must necessarily first respect it for what it literally is: the story of a couple's sexual awakening and the beauty of their erotic delights in one another.

KNOWING AND BEING KNOWN

Healthy sexual experience is about our soul expressing itself to another through the body's sight, touch, sound, movement, and scent. The ancient Hebrews called this special kind of communication "knowing," as in "Isaac knew his wife...and he was comforted" (Genesis 24:67 ESV).

That passage from the book of Genesis is revealing because it tells us that we nurture our souls by making them known. We wouldn't be going too far to say then that healthy sexual intimacy is a source of life to the soul, one of those good things that God will not with-hold from those who love Him.[3] Although single believers do not have a sexual partner, they are no less sexual beings than those who do. Therefore, single or married, most of us long for healthy sexual expression consistent with the state of life to which we are called. The overwhelming majority of us are either presently having sex with someone or are preparing ourselves for that eventuality. We want to know how to do it in a way that touches our soul.

However, like most good things, healthy sexuality does not just happen; we must purposefully cultivate it. If we want our soul to "know" another soul, our body must learn how to speak and under-stand the soul's language. Our touch must become more than mere pressure on our beloved's body; it must become like words of the spirit that our loved one can hear in the depth of his or her being. We must learn to play the instrument of our soul, namely, our body.

In other words, our soul needs a body in order to speak to God. That's why, when we pray, we naturally desire to lift our hands, kneel, make the sign of the cross, clap, dance, or do those things that our particular spiritual family uses to communicate with God. Spiritual life doesn't get very far until it connects with our body and learns to use the body as an instrument of devotion and praise.

When our soul is able to express itself through our body, we say that we are uninhibited. That is an important quality in giving and receiving sexual pleasure. In fact, in both our erotic and spiritual lives, we must learn how to let go, to surrender to the currents of spirit within, and thus to experience delight and release in the presence of our beloved.

Believers were so overcome with delight at Pentecost that the onlookers thought they were drunk! How often has that ever happened to us? Like a shy lover, we may be reluctant to surrender ourselves to such intense joy. However, that reluctance can keep us from the mysti-cal connection with our Creator for which our soul hungers.

Like any lover, God delights in our physical response. He warns us not to be drunk with wine, which leads to excess, but to be filled with the Holy Spirit.[4]

This reference to wine and intoxication is telling. When one is drunk, he loses a measure of control and inhibition. Although one should not misuse this passage to justify mindless behavior in the name of God, surely it is an invitation to delight both now and in the world to come!

WHY WINE?

Many Evangelical Christians, especially those from churches with roots in the American Southeast, are teetotalers. This stance, which became fully developed during the Prohibition, had been gaining ground since the Civil War for good reasons.

The peoples on the American frontier suffered from violence and deprivation that were often caused by alcoholism. They used their stills to make numerous kinds of brews, to which generations of men became addicted. These addicts often became financially irresponsible, incestuous, and given to fits of rage that left people wounded or dead. The gospel delivered many Southern and frontier people from the sorrow and devastation they had learned to associate with alcohol.

These were people who seldom (or ever) witnessed a family drinking a glass of wine with dinner as they might have in Europe. For them, all alcohol led to sin and sorrow, and they wanted no part of it. (As an aside, the same thing could be said about how people on the frontier experienced sex. For many women, sex was unbearably degrading. They too often experienced it as an act of dominance, likely to result in a pregnancy for which they would be blamed.)

In the great post–Civil War revivals, Jesus seemed to be delivering everyone. He was particularly delivering women from the male vices of drink and promiscuity that had made their lives so brutal. The church was a safe place for women and children, and even some men became "good." To be "good," however, meant walking away from the largely male vices that had led to abuse—particularly alcohol.

There was one obvious problem with this, however—the sacrament of Holy Communion. How could one be a Christian without observing the core sacrament that Jesus commanded His followers to observe? The dilemma caused much controversy.

Thomas Welch, a communion steward in his New Jersey church, perfected his pasteurization process for grape juice to produce "an unfermented sacramental wine." Southern Evangelicals' problem was solved. For the first time, people could maintain juice in an unfermented state. Since Evangelicals had come to view Communion as a symbolic gesture anyway, the exact nature of the elements used in the rite were not as crucial for them as it was for older and more traditional Christian groups. For all these reasons, first the Methodists and then many other Protestant groups in the United States began to substitute wine with unfermented grape juice.

This is not the place to argue about the appropriateness of using grape juice in Communion. Personally, I have no issue with it. In fact, I serve a congregation where this is the norm. I also understand the reasons for using grape juice, especially where people have had issues with alcoholism. Still, we should note that in both the Old and the New Testaments, God instructed believers to drink wine as an act of worship.

It will not do to say that the wine was nonfermented grape juice, not only because of the late development of the pasteurization process but because St. Paul clearly rebukes believers for getting drunk at Communion. Furthermore, the Old and New Testaments' warnings about drunkenness would be completely unnecessary if God's followers were forbidden to drink fermented beverages.

Clearly then, the Bible treats wine, fermented and potentially intoxicating, as a vital ingredient of worship.

To understand why God instructed us to drink wine in worship, we must try to put ourselves into the environment of the ancient world. As I mentioned earlier, distillation was unknown before medieval times. The development of stills, which allowed people to make liquors and other powerful kinds of alcoholic brews, changed everything.

Getting drunk no longer required one to consume vast quantities of liquid; a glass or two of fortified and distilled drinks sufficed.

Nonetheless, even in the ancient world it was *possible* to get drunk on wine. Then, as now, wine, like finances, firearms, and sex, was dangerous. Indeed, all activities involving life and energy are dangerous. Therefore, a part of becoming a mature, self-governed, covenant-keeper was and is learning how to manage power, energy, and other dangerous things. Spirituality is one of them. It is not safe. It requires maturity.

Both the Old and the New Testament depict wine as a substitute for blood. Redemption and forgiveness require sacrifice and death, so the Bible institutes ways of worship that include symbols and reminders to make us deeply aware of this reality.

People also drank wine at social occasions to remember that they were united by blood and that maintaining their community might require the shedding of blood. Shedding blood was a serious thing; it had to be regulated and controlled. One could not just decide to shed blood, even of an animal. Blood is life; it must be respected.

Because things related to the wellspring of life are often dangerous, adults had to learn how to manage them. An adult could use wine but not misuse it. He could drink, but he must not get drunk. He could have sex but only with his wife. He could fight to defend his family and country; if he killed the enemy in the process, he was blameless. However, he must not slay his neighbor in a fit of rage; if he did, he was put to death. The passions of life must not control the covenant man; a covenant man must govern his passions. There is a time and place for everything under the heavens, including lovemaking and feasts. These are times to dance, laugh, drink wine, and play.[5] Even then, however, one was responsible for his actions and how those actions might affect others.

So all things related to the wellspring of life required mature management. Such things were dangerous and were not for children; they required instruction and self-governance. That's what maturity meant and what it means still.

Covenant people had to learn how to become mature. Maturity doesn't just happen on its own.

In the ancient world, people often drank wine to seal an agreement. In this ceremonial act, each partner of the covenant affirmed the maturity of the other. By drinking wine together, each was saying to the other, "I can trust you to keep your promise in spite of your shifting moods and changing circumstances. I can trust you to approach the wellsprings of my life—my goods, my family, and my very being. This wine, which looks so much like blood, represents my very life. I have come to believe that you are responsible enough to manage it."

Good sex also requires the deep trust of covenant. Hurting someone is easy during sex. We can wound our partner's spirit. However, in sex, we can also create new life. We can light a fire inside others that will make them see themselves in entirely new ways. We can encourage their self-confidence or destroy it. We can point people Godward or push them toward evil. In short, having sex with someone is to entrust that person with the wellsprings of our lives. Therefore, we must make sure that our partner knows how to manage such power and danger before we allow access to our hearts.

Addiction is not a good sign that a partner can handle so great a trust because an addicted person treats sensation as an end to itself. The sensation of a sacramental experience becomes more important than the covenant it is meant to signify. We rightly tend to turn away from such a person.

Our Lord ended His earthly ministry by pouring out His life's blood to save us. He proved Himself trustworthy to be the guardian of our lives. We can trust Him.

He also trusts us. That is why He began His ministry the way He did.

Through His miracle at Cana, Jesus was letting us know that He does not expect us to misuse potentially life-giving but dangerous experiences. He expects us to learn how to exercise mature management of adult things. So He turns the water into wine. He trusts the people at the feast; He believes they will enjoy their drink without abusing it. He trusts the couple in the hut; He knows they will enjoy each other without violating the deep trust they have just pledged one to another in God's name.

When the festivities are over, He knows the villagers will return to their work, harvest their grain, and feed one another. He knows that when the honeymoon ends, the lovers will return to everyday life and raise their new family. They will face the chores, difficulties, and blessings of molding their children into adults.

Today, however, is a feast day. A young man and a young woman are naked on their bed, overwhelmed by their awe of erotic love. Their time is precious, their erotic joys sacred. They need privacy to develop their delight and to nurture their young love. So our Lord's mother takes note that there is no wine.

She looks at the One who came that we might have life, and then she looks at the wedding attendants. With a smile she says, "Whatever He says to you, do it." [6]

She knows what He will do because she knows Him.

Two

GROW UP!

I was facing a room full of clergy, all of whom had committed some sort of sexual impropriety. Now, after years of recovery, they wanted to share their stories.

I knew there was a lot of wisdom in that room and a lot of pain.

Most of the men and women were from holiness denominations, which teach a doctrine called "entire sanctification." Although on this occasion I was there as a therapist and not as a pastor, I began by acknowledging their teaching.

"Well," I said, "for years I have wondered about what you guys mean by 'entire sanctification.' Now I think I understand! You mean prepubescence. You believe that becoming holy means becoming a little boy or little girl again, at least where sexuality is concerned. You can't imagine a holy man or a holy woman being thoroughly aroused and enjoying good sex. That implies that nobody in this room is holy and is never likely to be!

"So," I continued, "wouldn't it have been better if your parents had just shot you before you went through puberty?"

For a moment I thought I had gone too far. Then, as everyone started laughing, I knew I had hit a nerve. Actually, everyone in that room wanted to be a holy person. The problem was that they had defined holiness in a way that doomed them to failure.

Like everyone else, those pastors were sexual beings. Their denial of sexuality had not helped them become holy; it had only left them unprepared to deal with temptation. Their attempts at being children meant that they didn't learn how to manage their sacred longings for erotic life.

Whatever holiness is, it cannot be a denial of creation. If sexuality is part of the created order, God Himself is responsible for it. This implies that to be holy, we must accept and manage our sexuality, not deny it. It implies that we must embrace puberty rather than repudiate it, that we must learn to be righteous adults rather than perpetual adolescents.

ADULTHOOD IS NOT AUTOMATIC

Many years ago, I was with a well-known preacher at a restaurant. While looking at the menu, he became enthralled with a picture of a sundae with scoops of ice cream covered with syrup, fruit, and nuts. He decided that he had to have it!

But when the waitress brought him the sundae, he became visibly upset. He couldn't stop complaining, even after he plunged into the dessert. Bite after bite, he pontificated about false advertisement, poor service, and the demise of civilized life. Finally, he called the waitress.

"Miss," he growled, "I am exceedingly disappointed!" (He really did say "exceedingly.") "When I see a picture like this, I expect to get a sundae like this one" (he was thumping the menu with his finger), "not one with holes between the scoops of ice cream!"

A few minutes later, his waitress returned with a very large sundae, saying nothing about the fact that he had already consumed half of the sundae he had returned. He broke into a big smile, thanked her, and then dived into the gigantic sundae. He ate every last bite of it as he instructed everyone at the table to always stand up for himself, not to accept poor service, and so forth.

I listened to him the following night as he appealed to a large crowd about how to become followers of Jesus. I kept wondering how following such a man could possibly help anyone. Spiritual leaders should at least be responsible adults.

Wives and husbands should be able to expect the same from their partners. Childish people make poor lovers.

Some years ago, a book was released about how to live with Peter Pan. Its main idea was that Peter Pan is cute in the movies, but he is really difficult to live with. A little boy is a precious human being when he really is little. When he is 40 years old, however, a little boy is a pain in the neck.

When boys or girls don't grow up, others have to keep taking care of them. These others are often spouses who marry their darling playmate, have a lot of fun, and then begin to mature as responsibilities come along. Sometimes, the responsible spouse takes a while to realize that his or her playmate has not been maturing at the same pace.

So we have plenty of old fools in the world—Peter Pans—who manage to squander every opportunity to grow up. The years come and go, each one offering unique opportunities to reflect, mature, and expand. But to each one, the overgrown children keep saying "no thanks." They remain children or adolescents or teenagers housed in aging bodies.

Adulthood does not always come with age. Although physical maturation comes automatically, social, emotional, intellectual, and spiritual growth is a result of our decisions and conscious adaptations to life.

So what exactly is adulthood? Perhaps as good a definition as any is simply "the ability to manage our resources in a way that contributes to our well-being and that of those for whom we are responsible."

None of us mature at the same pace in every area of life. We can manage one area of life well while failing at others. For example, a person can be financially responsible and sexually irresponsible at the same time. One can be a good parent and not a good husband. One can be a good preacher and a lousy friend. Different parts of life require different skills, all of which must be learned and developed.

In the summer of 2004, my wife, Trish, suffered a devastating brain aneurysm. Because her life was in danger, I quickly had to make some crucial decisions. My first decision was to select a competent neurosurgeon. The hospital suggested Dr. Albuquerque whom, they claimed, was one of the nation's best.

I signed an authorization for the famous neurosurgeon to open my wife's skull. I put her brain in his hands; mine were incapable of doing what had to be done.

To this day I don't know anything about Dr. Albuquerque's religion, politics, or taste in literature. We probably differ on all those points. What I do know is that I made the right decision. He proved to be a highly competent neurosurgeon, and he saved Trish's life.

I am convinced that the prayers of godly people sustained Trish and me during those dark days. So I certainly mean no disrespect when I say I would have resisted any of them had they attempted to do Dr. Albuquerque's job. None of them were qualified to perform neurosurgical procedures. A godly character does not make one competent in all areas of life.

The Bible says, "In all your getting, get understanding."[1]

"Understanding" means discovering what "stands under." Financial understanding is about discovering the attitudes, behaviors, and habits that contribute to (or erode) financial well-being. To have an understanding of parenting is to know what is necessary to guide a child from infancy to adulthood. Social understanding is knowledge about making and maintaining acquaintances, friendships, and communities. *Sexual* understanding is knowledge about male and female anatomy, a sense about how men and women experience sexual desire, a grasp of sexual etiquette, an awareness of what is or is not appropriate in different circumstances, and so forth.

Maturity is about applying the understanding we have gained and acknowledging the areas of life for which we lack understanding. We do not all need to understand neurosurgery, but most of us do need sexual understanding.

The problem is that sexual understanding does not just happen. Like all forms of knowledge, we must seek after it and then intentionally apply what we have learned to our lives.

We don't fault the adolescent for his sexual awkwardness. However, we assume that mature men and women will know how to manage their sexual issues with respect, wisdom, and experience. Despite all the old stories we heard in our high school locker rooms and even what we think is common sense, sexual maturity requires us to grow in knowledge, to deliberately adopt that knowledge, and through trial and error, to gradually learn to manage our sexuality for our own benefit and for the benefit of our beloved.

All of us are sexual by nature. However, human love requires more than mere nature. Creating culture and community requires us to cultivate and manage nature. Mature people do not just settle for what comes naturally.

In other words, maturity involves turning a raw product into a finished product.

An old Communion prayer illustrates what I mean:

> We thank Thee, Lord God, King of the universe, for this bread, which Thou hast created and which human hands have prepared. It shall be for us the body of Christ.

The prayer expresses the belief that worship is an interactive experience between God and His people. God gives us the products of nature—our talents, possessions, and personalities. He expects us to develop these natural products and to offer them back to Him. Then He promises to bless what we have crafted for His service. We cannot make wheat; only God can do that. However, we can make bread from the wheat He gives us. Only He can bless that bread so that it becomes capable of feeding not only our natural self but also our spiritual self. (That is also the principle behind tithing—and any other sacramental action for that matter.)

By the time Trish needed him, Dr. Albuquerque had been developing his raw products of finger dexterity and high intelligence for many years. That's how he had become a skilled surgeon. Without a doubt, some people have the same natural abilities as his, but they use them to assemble ships inside bottles. Those people developed their raw products into very different finished products than Dr. Albuquerque did.

A naturally talented cook has the ability to become a great chef. However, actually becoming a chef usually requires a mentor; an exposure to the potential of meats, vegetables, herbs and spices; and some years of experience. It doesn't just happen.

Sexuality is like that too. We must intentionally develop it to make it the blessing that we hope for it to be in our lives. Though everyone with genitals has the ability to be sexual at some level, this natural ability is a raw product; it is not a finished product.

AROUSAL

In the famous Seinfeld episode called "The Contest," the characters of the show placed bets in how long they could go without acting out sexually. Kramer of course was the first loser. Unfortunately, he looked out of his high-rise apartment window and saw a naked woman in the building across the street. He promptly excused himself from the room. When he returned, he put his money down on the counter.

Part of becoming a sexually mature person is learning how to manage arousal. Kramer didn't qualify! Arousal is a basic physical response to the presence of a sexual stimulant. Though it announces the potential for sex, it does not require any action, only a choice: to move toward or away from the stimulus.

Adolescents experience spontaneous arousal as an immediate and irrepressible need. They feel as though they must do something about this feeling—soon! However, adults learn to process arousal and to make intelligent choices about what to do with it.

Mature people acknowledge their arousal as their own; they realize they experience it merely as a natural response to the presence of a desirable person. It requires no action and calls for no blame. Like the wind that blows, arousal is just nature. The way we manage our arousal makes it creative or destructive, loving or abusive, a gift or harassment.

Certainly a mature Christian will not attach any undue spiritual significance to a moment of spontaneous arousal. Good people, holy people, people with functioning hormones get aroused. The question is, does the arousal overwhelm and highjack their thoughts, or is it merely a passing awareness of the sexual potential of a given situation? Mature people discover ways of dealing with their arousal and form conscious decisions about how to respond. Dealing with arousal is each person's own responsibility.

Of course, managing our sexuality is not merely about imposing limits upon ourselves and others. It's also about cultivating and acquiring sexual awareness, sensitivity, and skill. Although some people are naturally more at ease with their sexuality than others, sexual maturity always requires an intentional development of what nature gives us.

Sexual maturity is like mastering gymnastics, acquiring a language, driving a car, or developing a musical skill. It requires knowledge, experience, and time. It doesn't come naturally.

Someone said that the guitar is the world's easiest instrument to play but the most difficult one to master. Some musicians might disagree with the statement, but most will understand what the guy meant. You can learn in an afternoon how to play three chords and strum along to a simple melody. To play Bach or a bolero, however, takes years of training and practice. The young guitarist is understandably proud of himself as he strokes the chords and makes music. He is not, however, an Andrés Segovia or a Chet Atkins. To play a duet that brings the house down, he must master his instrument, gain a deep knowledge of the music, soulfully express his emotions, and show respect for his fellow musicians. No one is born with the ability to do all of this; it must be developed.

THE EXCEPTIONAL IS NOT THE NORM

Bill and Pamela Burton had been married for two years when his company downsized. They were fairly good managers of their money, but after three months, things were getting pretty tight. The long picture looked good: An old boss had called to say that he would need someone with Bill's computer skills in about four months. But they would be in financial problems by then.

Just a few days after the call from his old boss, Bill got another call. This one was from a buddy with whom he had worked in the company that had downsized. His friend told him that a few jobs had opened up with a company in Alaska that repaired oil pipelines. They had an opening for a temporary job—it would only last eight weeks—but the pay was good.

After discussing it with Pamela, Bill called to ask his friend to e-mail him the application. He was hired within the week and was off to Anchorage.

The work was interesting, and Bill was glad to have the income. During the day, he hardly had time to think, so the first few weeks passed quickly. As time passed, however, the nights started getting very lonely. He and Pamela e-mailed and talked on the phone, but after the first couple of weeks, their absence from one another started bothering them.

Three weeks before their scheduled reunion, Pamela received a surprise bonus at work. By the time she got home that day, she had decided how she would use the money. She would fly to San Francisco, meet Bill, and they would stay in a nice hotel for three nights. Bill was delighted when she told him about her plan. They talked every night on the phone about their little vacation. They even sent racy e-mails about all they would do to one another in San Francisco.

When the big day finally arrived, Bill flew to San Francisco. Pamela had arrived just a half hour before, and she met him at the gate as he got off the plane. She told him she had no baggage. Everything she needed was in her small carry-on bag.

When they talked about it later, they laughed and wondered how they had ever made it to their hotel room. They were so hungry for one another that they didn't mind showing it.

They had a wonderful time in San Francisco, filling the three days with good food, loving talk, and lots of delightful sex.

Four years later, they went to a marriage counselor. As they both put it, the sizzle had gone out of their sex life.

They told their story about San Francisco on their third visit to the counselor. The therapist noticed that they told the same story and that they looked into one another's eyes as they told it. He could see that they were still very much in love.

They were shocked when the therapist told them that nothing was seriously wrong with their marriage except that their days in San Francisco had been special. They had been set up for great sex. Furthermore, though the exact circumstances would not be repeated, they could plan another erotic vacation. That would give them something to anticipate. However, the exceptional *is* exceptional because it is different from the day-to-day. Feasts are not everyday meals; a vacation is not everyday life.

Sex like Bill and Pamela enjoyed in San Francisco does not become a twice-a-week occurrence, despite what the movies depict. Couples have bills to pay, long hours of work, disputes about what color to paint the living room, and a hundred other small things that diminish their attention. They should enjoy having sex even in the midst of normal life, of course. However, sex is rarely as spectacular as when it has our full attention. We write poems and songs about our special romantic and sexual moments, but the mundane responsibilities of everyday life actually do more to build our marriages and families. Special erotic occasions are treats, not the essence of marriage and family life.

I don't mean to diminish the importance of having good sex. I certainly don't want to claim that sex isn't good except on vacation! I merely want to point out that exceptional sex usually happens when people have been anticipating it, when they can focus intently on one another, and when they are rested and full of energy.

A wise couple plans such occasions!

GROWING OLDER

A lady told me once that she first discovered that her mom and dad had sex when she was about 13. She awoke one night to hear her mother sighing and groaning. Alarmed, she started running toward her parents' bedroom. She was about to open their door when she heard her parents giggle and say something like, "We're still good!"

She found it all rather mysterious at first. Then it hit her! *My mom and dad were having sex!* she said to herself.

She ran to her older sister's bedroom to tell her what had just happened.

"Oh, my Lord!" her sister replied. "Oh, my Lord!" Then her sister pretended to gag. "To think that those old carcasses have been down there flopping around just turns my stomach!"

"My sister and I spent the rest of the night laughing and talking about sex," my friend said. "I think we were really delighted to know that our 'old' mom and dad—they were probably in their early forties—still made love. It made us feel secure. It also helped us to accept our own developing sexuality.

"They have been gone now for a few years. I never told my parents about what had happened. It would have embarrassed them. But a few weeks ago, my sister called and asked me if me and my husband still flop our old carcasses around together. I indignantly replied, 'You bet we do!'

"After getting off the phone, I wondered how my own life would have turned out if I had not known that my very spiritual parents were also very sexual people. It really was a gift!"

People don't stop being sexual just because they get old.

My uncle used to love to tell a story about the time he asked my great granddad about sex. "Poppy," he asked, "how old is a man when he stops wanting a woman?"

"Hmm, don't know," Poppy Jordan replied. "You gotta ask somebody older than me."

Poppy was 94!

The truth is, we are sexual beings all our lives.

Of course, the way we express sexuality changes over time. If we don't know that, we can become angry and afraid of the changes of life. That's when we often make a real mess of things.

I had a friend whose marriage became more difficult as time went by. John just couldn't stop longing for the old days, when he and Mary Ann had been teenage lovers. They had become parents, and his wife had become a seasoned and wise woman, but he still wanted to see her as the naive girl with the ponytail in the backseat of his dad's Buick!

Every era of life calls for different kinds of understanding and adaptation. We have babies who become toddlers, adolescents, and then teenagers. They leave home, get careers, and get married. We become grandparents. Our body changes, culture changes, and our spouse changes. A successful life is one that is constantly able to adapt to these changes gradually and appropriately.

All women know that menopause changes life. Menstruation stops. Hormones reconfigure. Personality shifts. Women adapt.

Many men seem not to realize that something similar happens to them.

However, masculine sexuality changes as we age too. Men's changes are usually more gradual and subtle than women's, so men often ignore them as long as they can. When a man finally begins to notice the changes, he is often shocked and dismayed. He may experience what seems to be a sudden sense of diminished sexual drive. He may begin to long for a romantic connection with a new partner. He may try to overcompensate for his waning sexual drive, acting like a supernova before the fire goes out.

A man may frantically look for a way to turn back the clock. How? A new woman? A youthful car? Testosterone injections? What?

The fact is, many older men and women enjoy the best sex of their lives in their later years. Life makes them slow down. If erections take longer and are less dependable, lovemaking has to be about something more than erections and ejaculations. If natural lubrication has become an issue and the couple is forced to use commercial lubricating products, their discovery may lead them to explore other kinds of marital aids. If intercourse becomes difficult, they may discover that mutual masturbation or oral sex can open up a new level of intimate awareness to one another. In short, as we age, sexual fulfillment requires learning and experimentation, just as it does earlier in life.

If couples compensate for one another's physical changes and treat one another with dignity and grace, their difficulties usually prove to be temporary and are easily overcome. Lovemaking becomes as much about touch and tenderness as about orgasm. As a result, orgasms can become quite intense.

As in any stage of life, good sex in older years requires a deliberate search for new knowledge, openness to express one's desires without a fear of shame, and a willingness to accept what life has brought.

A WORD FROM TOLSTOY

Tolstoy's short stories contain some of the most powerful and profound thoughts in world literature. His novels are the size of telephone books and cause hernias. However, his short stories are just delightful. One of my favorites is "Family Happiness."

In the story, a widower marries a much younger rural Russian woman. After a couple of years of wonderful married bliss, they move to the Russian capital of St. Petersburg, where she encounters the social life of the Russian upper crust. She becomes popular in those circles and tries to attend every dance and party the city offers.

In time, the couple must return to their provincial home. The husband, older and more settled, is ready to return to his ordinary life. His wife, however, grieves the loss of her newly won sophistication. She becomes depressed and moody, which alienates her from her husband. The next few years of the couple's life are difficult and strained.

One evening, the husband goes to his children's bedroom to see that they are safely in bed. When he enters the room, he sees his wife hovering over his sons. The moonlight silhouettes her against the window behind the bed, so he stops to take in the scene. Suddenly he watches as she slowly makes the sign of the cross over her children. Then she turns to see her husband standing in the doorway.

In that moment, Tolstoy says, as they look at each other, they realize that their love has always been there and always will be. They also realize that each stage of life has its own joys and its own difficulties. When we cling to any stage of life, we lose the joys that we could experience in the next stage and fail to preserve the joys of the stage we must, at any rate, leave behind.

The wife joins her husband at the door and takes his hand. They close the door of the room where their children sleep. They then walk down the long hall to their own room, happy and together.

Three

GOOD SEX

WHEN BODY AND SOUL COME TOGETHER

Shawna was frustrated with her husband, Larry.

"He treats sex like a drive-by shooting! Last week, when he finally wanted to have sex, I was glad. I thought, *Wow—it's about time!* So I actually got quite worked up.

"I shouldn't have bothered. It was all over before I knew what happened. He was like Julius Caesar: He saw, he came, and he conquered. When he had his orgasm, he kissed me on the cheek and was soon snoring away. I could have shot him!"

Her "drive-by assassin" had made a fundamental mistake; he had treated sex as a mere physical release.

His wife needs much more. Likely, the next time Speedy Gonzales starts acting amorous, he's going to face some icy resistance. Of course, he probably won't have any idea what her problem is!

Laura had the opposite problem. She had been ashamed to tell her husband, Boice, that she longed for some no-holds-barred, sweaty, and very physical sex. One night, she suddenly let it all loose and started moaning and thrashing about. Boice sat up in the bed and yelled, "What in God's name are you doing!"

49

He then gave her a lecture about "controlling her carnality." He married her, he said, because he thought she was interested in spiritual things. (She was leading a Bible study when he met her.) He had thought she would make an ideal wife and help him raise a good family.

"Hasn't sex been all right as it is?" he asked. "Haven't we had wonderful and intimate times? Why do you want to ruin it by acting like a porn star?"

When she told me about their argument in their first session as a couple, she protested, "It's not like that. I love our tender times. It's just that I don't think sex always has to be so weighty and deep. Sometimes I just want to let go and enjoy myself. Why is he trying to make me feel like a whore for just feeling sexual? It makes me not want to have sex with him at all."

Believe it or not, these two couples' sexual difficulties are related. They are rooted in the way the couples think about their souls and their bodies. That's why, the more I came to know them, the more I realized they both needed a theology lesson.

HERESY CAN RUIN YOUR SEX LIFE!

The great medieval theologian Thomas Aquinas taught that God appointed human beings to a unique place in the universe. We are not angels, which are spirits without bodies. Neither are we animals, which are bodies without spirits. We are incarnational creatures; that means we have both a body and a spirit. Furthermore, our body and spirit are not separate components of our being. They are interdependent. What happens to our spirit affects our body, and what happens to our body affects our spirit.

By treating Shawna as though she were a mere body, Larry was guilty of "animalism," or denying his wife's spirit. By treating Laura as a mere spiritual being, Boice was guilty of "angelism," or denying his wife's physicality.

As Christians, Boice and Larry needed to relate to themselves and to their wives as incarnational beings, as creatures that are "ensouled" bodies and embodied spirits.

Aquinas came up with his definitions of "animalism" and "angelism" as he reflected on one of Christianity's central teachings: the doctrine of the incarnation, or the belief that God became a man. That doctrine leads to another one: the resurrection of the body. Christians confess both of these beliefs every time they recite the Apostle's and the Nicene Creeds, the two great confessions of their faith.

Isn't it amazing how we can so piously confess such powerful truths about human life and then ignore what they imply? Unfortunately, however, we can hold inconsistent belief systems or confess one thing while actually living another. Many believers are doing precisely that where sexuality is concerned.

To believe that God became a man—not appeared to be a man, but actually became a man—and that He now eternally inhabits a human body implies a high view of our physical life. Add to this the doctrine of the resurrection of the body, and we would think we could not possibly disdain our natural appetites.

So what gives? Why do so many Christians fail to cherish their bodies? I think it's because we fail to correctly define the word "soul."

A PRAYER FOR THE BATHROOM

Many years ago I was asked to do my first house blessing.

When I got to the house, I reviewed the ceremony in the car with my wife. I read over the prayers for the entryway and the kitchen, the bedrooms and the garden with appreciation. However, I drew the line at the prayer for the bathroom.

"I refuse to pray over a toilet!" I said to my wife. "Only a bunch of crazy Anglicans would write a prayer for a bathroom!"

But for some reason, when we actually went through the ceremony, I found myself reading the bathroom prayer before I had a chance to think about it.

O Holy God, in the incarnation of Your Son, our Lord, You made our flesh to be the instrument of Your self-revelation.

Give us a proper respect and reverence for our mortal bodies, keeping them clean and fair, whole and sound; that, glorifying You in them, we may confidently await our being clothed with spiritual bodies, when that which is mortal is transformed by life; through Jesus Christ our Lord. Amen.

As I read that prayer, I had an epiphany. God was interested in our mortal bodies! He wanted us to keep them clean and presentable. I had acted as if God were interested only in some invisible part of our being.

Not long afterward, I reread the first five books of the Bible. I was amazed to see how much God cared about food, cleanliness, and appearance. Clearly, having a low view of our body was as incompatible with the Bible as having a low view of our spirit.

Larry needed to connect with his wife's inner being because she is a spiritual creature. Boice needed to enjoy his wife's body because she is a physical creature.

Both Larry and Boice need a definition of "soul" that makes them aware that we are beings with both bodies and spirits. Unfortunately, like many people, they have been defining "soul" in ways that are more compatible to ancient Gnosticism than to either Judaism or Christianity.

WHAT IS A SOUL?

If you ask someone to define the word "soul," you will likely hear one of two answers. One answer is that the soul is an eternal but invisible substance that resides within the human body. A less common response will be that "soul" is another word for "the entire person." The second answer implies that the body and its desires are part of our spiritual life; the first answer implies that the body is a hindrance to spiritual life.

Boice wants sex from time to time. However, because he fancies himself to be a spiritual man, he fears becoming carnal and bestial. He wants his sexual life to be upright, holy, safe, godly, and spiritual. Laura, on the other hand, wants to experience her body—to abandon herself to physical sensation and delight. She wants incarnational sex.

The truth of the matter is that Laura scares Boice! He is so disconnected from his physical body that he has no idea what she is doing. When she moaned and moved the way she did that night he so sternly rebuked her, she seemed to him to be out of control, even animalistic. He admitted to me later that he thought she might be possessed!

Obviously, Boice was raised to live as much as possible as though he had no body. He has been taught that this is the way to spiritual life. Imagine then how amazed he was when I told him that I thought his wife was much more spiritually mature than he was.

"Frankly," I told him as tenderly as I could, "I think of you as a scared little boy, at least where sex is concerned."

So did his wife. That's why I had to find a way to get through to him.

He had thought of himself as a spiritual giant because he was so interested in his soul. Was he ever surprised when I told him that according to the Bible, what he called a "soul" didn't even exist! Sexually speaking, he was more of a disciple of Plato than he was of Christ.

APOSTLE PLATO?

Many of the ancient Greek philosophers that influenced early Christians used the word "soul" to refer to the nonmaterial essence of a man. To these philosophers, one's soul was an eternal entity clothed with a material body. With training, one could learn to manifest his or her soul, but even so, a soul was rather like a condemned criminal. It might peek through the body from time to time, as through the windows of a prison, but it would not be completely free until death brought deliverance.

The prison in this metaphor is, of course, the body. If one adopts a Platonic view, then it makes perfect sense that a person who desires to be spiritual will want to transcend his or her physical being.

That is what happened to early Christians. They abandoned the Hebrew definition of "soul" and adopted the Greek one. They began to think of spiritual development as gradually distancing themselves from their bodies. Since Plato, cultured men had sought to become disembodied intelligence. From the third century onward, many Christians influenced by him hungered to become disembodied spirits, like Boice.

Boice wants what we call a "platonic" relationship with his wife. The word refers to the teachings of Plato's disciples about transcending bodily needs in order to grow one's soul. Usually we use the word to describe a relationship that is not sexual at all. That is not the case with Boice. He does want to have sex with his wife; he just wants it to be controlled and subdued. He wants the sex to be pleasurable enough to bring him release and connected enough to express love and kindness to his wife. What he doesn't want is to experience the full expression of erotic desire. He wants his horse to walk but never to gallop.

In his own mind, he is acting like a morally upright man by not allowing his body to overpower his reason. That is a mark of maturity in most respects, but in the safety and security of his own bedroom, with his own spouse, Boice can let his body break out in a run.

However, for many "spiritual" people, letting the body loose like that would be to betray the soul. After all, the body will soon be dead while the spirit lives forever.

That makes sense if the body is something other than a soul. Why should a spiritual person like Boice care about his body if it is merely a temporary abode for his "real" self—the soul? If anything, he ought to subdue his body so his soul can live and develop.

Boice is hardly alone. Western Christianity retains much of the early Greek influence on the faith. Indeed, that influence is so pervasive that many people think of it as part of the faith.

Solomon would certainly have been amazed!

The ancient Hebrew definition of "soul" was much like that implied by the headline of an English newspaper last century:

"Boat sinks in North Atlantic: three hundred souls lost!"

The headline informs us that 300 people died at sea. It does not mean that the invisible part of 300 people disappeared. The ancient Hebrews used the word similarly. To them, "soul" was not an invisible and abstract ghost. It was not an important letter, imprisoned inside a relatively unimportant envelope. The soul was the entire human being: body, mind, and spirit.

For the ancient Hebrews, then, the body is a part of one's soul. Therefore, we should treat our bodies with great respect. Far from being like an envelope, only incidentally related to the letter within, the body is the soul's skin; it is the soul's means of feeling and being felt.

To ancient Hebrews and to early Christians, the body was the soul's extension into the material world, and the soul was the body's extension into the spiritual world. To separate soul and body was impossible for them. After all, how could people confess to believe in the physical resurrection of the body if they actually longed for a spiritual liberation from the material world?

Soon after the New Testament era, however, Christian thinkers began to consider the body as an impediment to their spiritual quest. Many influential converts to the faith lacked Jewish teaching. They were philosophically trained Greeks. Naturally, they assigned meanings to biblical words that were more Greek than Hebrew.

One of the casualties of this theological shift was the Christian view of sexuality. After all, what more reminds us that we are physical beings than our appetites? Increasingly, the desire to eat, drink, and make love seemed to stand in the way of Christians' growing quest to become holy, which they had come to define as the quest to become disembodied spirits.

Leaders of the Christian church repeatedly denounced the repudiation of the material world. Nonetheless, the view had deeply infected the beliefs and practices of Christian believers.

It still does.

How many Christians have attempted to exorcize sexuality from their being, only to discover that we cannot cast out something that is an essential part of how our Creator formed us? The madness continues, though, until we learn the truth that we are, and will always remain, physical creatures. Unlike the ancient Greeks, Christians do not believe that the body is a prison from which we should seek release. It is not an envelope that we can safely discard once the letter is extracted. It is the temple of the Holy Spirit; it is our soul's eternal skin.

I haven't forgotten about Larry—the "drive-by assassin." Unlike spiritual Boice, Larry realizes that he is a physical being, and he is certainly aware that his wife has a body. He suffers from the opposite problem: He isn't aware of his spirit or Shawna's spirit.

St. Paul addressed this issue in his warnings to Christians in Corinth about not going to prostitutes. Strangely enough, the apostle didn't base his warning on moral grounds. Instead, he reminds believers that if they have sex with a prostitute, they will "take the members of Christ and make them members of a harlot." Because, he says, "he who is joined to a harlot is one body with her."[1]

Wow!

This means that the biblical basis for Christian morality cannot be that sexual pleasure is somehow beneath a spiritual person. No, a Christian is called to be moral because God trusts us to manage the spiritual life He gives to us. Therefore, when we act, we act in His name and for His sake. When we enter into agreements—and having sex with someone is one of life's most important agreements—God participates somehow and enters into that agreement with us.

It's a strange argument, admittedly. I certainly don't claim to understand it. However, St. Paul obviously believed that sexual actions have a spiritual impact on those who participate in them.

By treating Shawna as a mere body, Larry was dishonoring his wife. She had become a device to help him get to sleep. That not only dishonored Shawna but also displeased God.

The Bible says God didn't like Esau because he was a "profane" man, a man who didn't acknowledge the spiritual impact of his actions.[2]

Shawna was feeling the profanity of her husband's sex life. She wanted and deserved much more than that. After all, she is an eternal being, made in the image and the likeness of God.

My experience as a pastor and as a therapist has led me to believe that those who try to divide their soul from their body usually come to disaster. If they succeed at destroying their sexual desire, they destroy much of their zest for life. If they cannot extinguish their sexual desire, they lose much of their life's quality by wallowing in self-loathing. Either way, they reject God's creation in the name of the God they confess. It is a tragic mistake.

Both sexual addiction and sexual anorexia thrive among Christians because so many try to divorce their body from their soul. They fail to apply to their body and spirit the principle that the Lord Jesus applied to husbands and wives: "What God has joined together, let not man separate."[3]

A WORD ABOUT WORSHIP

Worship also suffers when we try to make it either too disembodied or too secular. If God has appointed human beings to be incarnational creatures who are both spiritual and material, then it stands to reason that He will meet with us in an incarnational way. He will not expect us to become disembodied spirits. Neither will He expect us to run from awe and transcendence.

When God met Moses on the mountain, He revealed the way He wanted us to worship. We are to arrange material things for worship in such a way that calls us out from everyday life and encourages us to set our sights on eternity. Churches are meant to be embassies of heaven, where we taste of the powers of the world to come. Worship is supposed to be the place where our attention gets arrested and focused upon God. We are to open our hearts so we will learn God's ways and then return to our everyday lives reminded that we are spiritual beings.

If we forget that we need a spiritual encounter, worship becomes performance. If we forget that we are material beings, worship becomes spooky and weird.

We are a package.

Body and soul come together.

Forever.

Four

MAY I HAVE YOUR ATTENTION?

FOCUSED AWARENESS IN SEX
AND SPIRITUAL LIFE

Trish and I had an interesting experience a few years ago. Our youth pastor invited us to spend the week at a camp with the church's teenagers. The camp would be about a 45-minute drive from Birmingham, Alabama, he said. When we agreed to go, I recalled hearing about a Shakespeare theater in Birmingham. I thought that one night we could slip away from the camp and take in some real culture.

I got a brochure and saw that on the night we were free, the theater would feature *Much Ado About Nothing*. So I bought an annotated edition of the play and began to read it, looking up all the old words and reading comments about the various lines. I also watched Emma Thompson and Kenneth Branagh's rendition on video.

When the big day arrived, I was ready. We changed from our old camp-meeting duds into evening clothes, left the camp, and drove into Birmingham. We had plenty of time to eat dinner before going to the theater, but I thought we should find the theater first anyway. So we looked at the little map on the back of a brochure.

The theater was located at the corner of First and Washington, the map said. We quickly found First Street. We also found Washington Street. We could not, however, find the corner of those two streets, where the Globe Theater was located. Something was wrong. We retraced our steps. Then we went back to the interstate. Finally we frantically ran the length of both streets.

The two streets never intersected. We could not find the Globe Theater.

By this time, Tricia and I were having an "intense discussion." I reflected on her map-reading abilities, she said something about my ancestry...those sorts of things. When that didn't help, I called into question the IQ of the mayor and members of the city council. How could this city not clearly mark such an important tourist location? Who ran the city of Birmingham, anyway?

This could have gone on longer if Trish had not happened to see one chilling word at the bottom of the brochure: "Mobile."

The word "Mobile" was a part of the address. At first, we just stared at the page. We couldn't believe it. We had been using a map of Mobile to find an address in Birmingham. Unfortunately, Mobile was a hundred miles away!

As it turns out, it is impossible to find a place in Birmingham when it is located in Mobile.

Here's what happened: I wanted to go see that play, so I was worked up. When I couldn't find the address, I just worked harder. Though I was lost, I didn't know I was lost. (That means that sincerity is no substitute for being right.) When I still couldn't find the address and knew I was running out of time, I started driving faster. When that didn't work out, I blamed my wife and her ability to read a map. (That didn't go far, since she is not what you might call "compliant.") Finally, when all else failed, I got angry with the city of Birmingham, blaming my environment.

In all that fury, it never dawned on me to check the accuracy of the anxious vision in my head against the map.

I was not paying enough attention. I was too focused on what

I already believed to be reality. When the reality in my head didn't match the reality in the world, I just tried harder to empower my private reality.

I have some bad news: We often try to have sex like that.

ZONING OUT

Sometimes, when we set a time and place for sex, we start making plans and then get worked up with anticipation. If all that fizzles, we wonder what went wrong. What often goes wrong is that we get too obsessed with the images and aims in our own heads. We fail to pay attention to what our partner is saying or doing. We don't look at what is happening around us. Because we are caught up with visions of grandeur and ecstasy in our heads, we fail to consult reality. We end up trying to find a place in Birmingham that is really in Mobile.

Gosh, that is embarrassing!

We can become so obsessed with our private reality that we get completely disconnected from the world outside our heads. Our friends and loved ones may not know it for a while, but eventually they discover that we are rarely listening to them. They start to catch on to our trick of responding to their key words and phrases with clichés. They stop pretending that we are connected to them.

Some of us live most of our lives that way, inside our own heads, daydreaming about nothing in particular. We often call it "zoning out," though the proper term is "dissociating." Whatever we call it, it is a big problem in relationships. It is particularly damaging to our sex lives.

Dissociation is not always bad, of course. One type of dissociation—shock—can even save our lives in dangerous situations.

For example, David Livingstone was once attacked by a lion and lived to tell the story! Twenty years after the attack, the famous nineteenth-century missionary wrote a fascinating account of his experience. He said that when the lion first attacked him, he felt a rush of fear. Then his fear was replaced by a sense of curiosity. He found himself observing the animal up close, even noting its scent.

He remained aware that the animal was tearing at his flesh, but he felt little pain, at least at the time.

The pain would come later. While the lion was actually ripping up his flesh, he felt so anesthetized that he became an interested observer.

When a lion is eating a person, the victim doesn't want to discuss Mozart, politics, or romance. She is about to die; what use to her are any of these things? No, a person in physical danger focuses on survival. Her mind ignores all facets of reality that do not work to help her survive. After the lion goes away, she may be bleeding profusely or even may have lost a limb, but she still will move steadily toward help without feeling any pain. When the danger is past, she will be able to weep or scream.

When we are in great danger, the ability to dissociate can save our lives. However, zoning out can also become a habit that diminishes our lives.

The same kind of process that keeps us functional while a lion is eating us also helps us block out emotional pain. For example, children numb themselves to abuse, fear, loss, and poverty. They learn how to function in a world they cannot control by numbing a part of what they perceive.

I once talked to a woman whose stepfather had often come into her room at night when she was little. "I just went away," she said. "It didn't really happen. I counted ceiling tiles and said nursery rhymes to myself while he did his thing."

A dissociate state like that is meant to be temporary. When the danger has passed, a person should feel the pain, acknowledge the trauma, and move on. However, some people can't do that. They turn their dissociation into a permanent habit, remaining numb to much of the richness of life as they stay focused on merely surviving. "The trade-off of a distorted awareness for a sense of security is, I believe, an organizing principle operating over many areas of human life."[1]

In other words, people who have a habit of zoning out are usually not in danger from anything except the anxiety in their own heads.

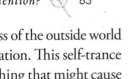

Nonetheless, they replace much of their awareness of the outside world with their own thoughts, emotions, and imagination. This self-trance works to keep their attention diverted from anything that might cause them discomfort and pain. Unfortunately, zoning out also numbs their awareness of joy, love, and beauty. Naturally, this hinders them from forming meaningful relationships with others.

Zoning out is particularly destructive to good sex.

As one man told me, "When my wife and I make love, I feel as though she is just going away somewhere. It's not that she's mad, sad, or glad. It's as though she's not even there!"

Unfortunately, he was probably right. For whatever reason, his wife has learned to "go away." She returns to herself when he finishes using her body. Afterward, if he should ask where she has been, she will likely be confused because she had been nowhere.

So zoning is an escape. Of course, everyone loses himself in deep thought sometimes. But intense thought has some objective. When someone dissociates, however—when he "zones out"—the place his awareness goes is not nearly as important as the stimulus from which it flees. The objective is simply to go away.

Sometimes that's funny.

I have an old home movie in which I caught a friend deliberately zoning out. His wife was a piano instructor who expected him to attend all of her student's recitals. I was sitting behind him in one of these recitals, recording his every move. I was filming him as he took his pen and made a mark on the program beside each child's name.

When little Jennifer finished her rendition of "Go tell Aunt Rhodie," John studiously checked off her name. He did the same thing after little Frederick, Elizabeth, and Anne played their songs.

To all appearances, he was the very picture of interest and decorum. However, when he saw my camera pointing at him, his little jerk and sheepish smile revealed that he had been somewhere else.

Poor John was just doing what he needed to do in order to survive sitting through a three-hour piano recital performed by grade-school kids. We can all sympathize.

Unfortunately, zoning out can be a much more serious problem. A child may learn to habitually dissociate to escape trauma or boredom by going away. Then, as she matures, she may not know to resist her tendency to zone out. At the first hint that some old danger or boredom may be returning, her conscious mind flees the scene, finding refuge in her inner world.

The trigger that sends her consciousness fleeing can be a word, a feeling, a scent, or most anything else. If she doesn't quickly break the spell, each mental image takes her consciousness yet deeper into herself. Soon she is cloistered within the caverns of her own self, leaping from one part of her private world to another, going nowhere in particular but staying away from the scary outside.

The movie *Click* explored the ramifications of zoning out. In the movie, the protagonist finds a remote control device that allows him to fast-forward his way through unpleasant things. He gets tired of hearing his children fuss, so he pushes the fast-forward button. He gets bored at work, so he pushes it again. His wife needs more foreplay for sex, so he fast-forwards to the good stuff. Before he realizes what has happened, he has rushed through his entire life. He misses everything.

Sadly, people do this all the time.

Habitual dissociation is the core of all addictions. Some addicts use drugs, some use sex, and others use religion as means to dissociate. However, some addicts are so good at self-trance that they need no help at all.

Regardless of whether chemicals or destructive behaviors are involved, zoning out is a form of abandonment of one's own self as well as one's family and friends. Therefore, when we try to relate to a person who is always zoned out, we are attempting to connect with someone who is simply not there.

Many people who come to therapy have spent more time dissociating from the outside world than they have interacting with it. They may not have been present long enough to read the signs that have marked the passing of their years or the erosion of their relationships.

It is a sad thing when people realize that they have not been experiencing their own life. They may be amazed that so much of their life has passed them by.

We pay a heavy price when we habitually zone out, particularly in sexual relationships. If sex is to be more than a mutual masturbation session in which each partner uses the other as an enhancement of his or her fantasies, lovers must learn how to direct their focus toward one another rather than going inside their own head.

In a "sexual trance," partners shut out the world around them and plunge into one another. In fact, when sex gets intense, this always happens. Our instincts take over, and our movements became soulful and fluid—like a dance. However, this is not a trance that shuts our lover out. It pulls him or her in more deeply than in any other kind of relationship.

Except one.

There is a reason we call the moment of spiritual enlightenment an "awakening." Worship is, after all, simply an intense focus on God, a deep awareness of His presence. Like our relationship with a lover, worship requires our full attention.

In fact, spiritual life is a constant call from God to awake us from our long sleep.

BEHOLD: THE AROUSAL OF SPIRIT

I love old words. I especially like them if my family and friends think they are slightly preposterous. I know, that's perverse. And people's patience with my old words has its limits. Even I know that I can't get away with sighing, "Alas, alas," or threaten to smite my enemies. I can't talk about fetching, feasting, or even expiring. Some old words really are dead.

We can express most of these concepts with modern words. However, in some cases, newer words truly can't express what needs to be said. That is especially true when it comes to a word like "behold."

Think about the modern words we use to replace "behold." "Look," "see," and "observe" all suffice (can we still say "suffice"?) to get a person to look where we are pointing. However, to behold is to do something much more profound than that.

"Behold" is what the child is trying to say in the cereal aisle at the supermarket: "Looky! Oh, Dad! Here! Oh—Captain Bob's Chocolate Bombs! There's a toy inside…Daaaaaaad! Loooook! Oh! OH!"

That works well enough for the hyper kid. Adults can't do that, however. They can't shake and yell, "Looky! Oh, oh, I want to tell you something so wonderful—oh, oh!"

Adults who talk that way are usually selling something on TV that costs $19.99.

We really don't have a modern word for "behold." Alas! The word "behold" seems utterly lost. (I couldn't resist!)

The King James Version of the Bible uses the word "behold" often. "Behold, the virgin shall conceive," the prophet Isaiah cries. "Behold, I bring you good tidings of great joy," the angel says to the shepherds at the nativity. "Behold what manner of love the Father has bestowed on us, that we should be called children of God," writes St. John in his epistle. Most importantly, John the Baptist cries out to us through the centuries, "Behold! The Lamb of God who takes away the sin of the world!"

The word "behold" comes from the Indo-European languages' earliest roots. In languages related to English, to behold something was to grasp and guard it. Only in English did it come to be connected to sight. Even in our language, to behold something means to mentally grasp it, to fix our attention on it. So it involves much more than mere seeing. To behold something is to focus our entire being upon it.

After all, the first part of the word "behold" is "be."

A DEFINITION OF BEING

The verb "to be" is the most irregular word in our language. The reason for this is that we have retained the primitive sounds we use to express it. When we conjugate the verb "to be," we make sounds that our ancestors made thousands of years ago. "Am," "was," "be," and "been" all have close relatives in the ancient languages of Sanskrit,

Hittite, Latin, and Greek. They are also deeply related to the modern languages of Europe and India. But beyond its linguistic ties, the verb "to be" is a mysterious entity in any language because it attempts to describe existence.

When President Clinton famously asked the federal prosecutors to define the word "is," he gave the late-night talk-show hosts material for weeks. However, had the lawyers actually given him an answer, they would have solved debates that go back thousands of years! Existence is mysterious and cannot be captured in words.

How does all of this relate to sex, you ask?

Well, among other things, good sex creates a heightened awareness of our own being. That's why arousal makes us feel so alive. It's why men and women often endanger their careers, reputations, and life itself to get sex. Few things can compare with its potential to connect us to raw existence. In fact, for secular people, sex seems to be the most intense way to taste sheer being.

They are mistaken, however. Sex is not being. It only reflects it, just as the moon reflects the sun. Sheer being is actually God Himself.

Being is the voice that cried to Moses from the burning bush and said, "I am! That is my name." These cryptic words were God's invitation to Moses not to study Him, nor to talk about Him, but to know Him. They were an invitation to come into relationship with life.

The same voice said to St. John the Revelator, "I am the Alpha and Omega...who is and who was and who is to come."

In these and many other passages, God reveals Himself to be the womb of existence, the fountain of being, the final answer as to why there is a single speck of dust in the universe rather than a vast, fathomless nothing.

By asking us to behold, God is calling to us to become aware of our connection to His continuous gift of existence.

Until we learn to respond to God's "behold," we are dead to the spiritual world, locked up in the narcissistic hell of our private universe. God's call awakens us to the possibility of life beyond ourselves.

That is what any relationship is: a shared sense of being.

Our friends and our lover are entitled to see the real person behind our private facades. We may politely invite our acquaintances into the "parlor" of our selves, but we must invite our lover into the whole of our selves. We sin against love, especially in the sexual moment, if we abandon our companion in favor of our own privately manufactured reality. Love is worthy of much more than that.

Behold!

Healthy sex is conscious sex; it is the quality of lovemaking experienced by two people who are fully focused on and aware of themselves and their partners. If we want to really connect with our beloved, become uninhibited in our physical, emotional, and spiritual response to their touch and truly make love, we have to cultivate a high level of awareness. We have to behold.

LEARNING HOW TO BEHOLD

I once heard about a lady who barely escaped bodily harm when, right at the moment her husband was ready to orgasm, asked him, "Honey, did you remember to take out the trash?"

We pride ourselves on our ability to multitask. However, no one wants to make love to someone while they are multitasking. Everyone who wants sex wants to experience it with someone who is paying attention! Therefore, learning to pay deep, focused attention is one of the great gifts we can give to our spouse.

We can start by increasing our focus on bodily sensations while having sex. Even important business deals should fade to the edge of our attention when we allow ourselves to truly feel our own pleasure.

Keeping our eyes open while having sex often increases a sense of intimacy and attention. If sexual partners look into one another's eyes while having sex—even while having orgasm—the connection between them can become nearly unbearably intense.

Many partners seem not to know that they can allow their arousal to plateau instead of continuing to orgasm. For example, if a couple becomes aroused but "pull back" before orgasm, they can remain in a state of arousal for some time. This allows them to talk, touch, embrace, and tease instead of concluding their time of lovemaking. Doing this requires time and a sense of leisure, but even if a couple can only experience it periodically, it can teach them to intensify their focus on one another in the more ordinary times.

Don't think about the chores while trying to have sex. The chores won't get done until you are finished having sex anyway, and someone is going to get very angry if they find out that they have been trying to have sex all by themselves!

Learning to pay attention will do more than increase the quality of your sex life. It will deepen all of your relationships. However, paying attention sometimes requires you to unplug from other things that vie for your attention.

LEARNING TO CONVERSE

Most of us know how to multitask. We can listen to our friends while thinking about income tax. We can drive through traffic while listening to the talk-show host. However, we simply can't do some things without paying close attention. We can't watch TV and read a great book at the same time. We can't drive and watch a DVD. And, as we have already established, if our spouse wants to make love, we should be willing to forget about everything else while we do it.

The problem is that we are used to interacting with modern life without paying much attention. We are ready to shift our focus toward any new stimulus, so we may not really know how to pay attention. That is why most modern conversation has become so superficial and disappointing.

Even learning to converse requires us to pay attention. We have to respond to what our friend says instead of using the time he is talking to formulate what we want to say. Sometimes, we even have to say something like this:

"To make sure I understand you, let me say in my own words what I believe you just said."

Few people will object to requests like that because everyone wants to be heard. If we give others a chance to correct our perception of their thoughts, they will nearly always respond well even if we disagree with them.

When we try to listen carefully to others, we will notice that our own heads are full of chatter. With practice, we can learn to turn off that chatter and focus on the voice of the person who is speaking to us. The person talking to us will notice the level of attention we are giving him or her.

We can ask our friends to tell us when they believe we are zoning out. I once told my congregation that if they thought I looked zoned out while they were trying to talk to me, they were free to ask me to repeat what they had just said. They could also ask me if I was fully present.

In time, I learned to say, "I am having a difficult time focusing right now. Please forgive me. Can we talk later?" Or, "Please run that by me again, I think I zoned out on you for a second. It's not your fault; I have problems with that sometimes."

No one ever seemed to be offended by my honesty—not even my patients at the clinic where I worked. People know at some level when we are not listening. They will appreciate our efforts to give them our best.

Dissociation can become a nasty habit. It takes a lot of work to break it. When we do, however, the changes in the quality of our relationships, in our power to think clearly, and in the level of sexual intensity we experience make it well worth the effort.

ETERNAL BEHOLDING

Here's a final word about beholding: None of us will truly and completely behold the beauty of the Lord until the day we pass from this life to the next. That will be the real moment of transformation, when we come into the state described by yet another old word: "beatitude," or eternal glorification.

When I was a little boy, the people in our little Pentecostal church used to sing a chorus about the bliss of eternal glory:

Just to behold His face
Just to behold His face
All I want up in heaven
Is just to behold His face

That is how human beings will be fully transformed into com-
panions of God—by eternally beholding His face. We will not fully
experience that in this life, for "now we see in a mirror, dimly."[2] However, even in this life we can experience glimpses of God. That is the
very essence of spiritual life: looking for God because He is looking
for us, and once finding Him, fixing our attention firmly on Him.

Five

THIS IS MY BODY

THE IMPORTANCE
OF INTIMACY

A few years ago, Trish gave me a unique gift for my birthday. Inside a beautifully wrapped box, I discovered a gift certificate for dance lessons for the two of us!

Through the years I had complained about how our denomination preached against dancing. That foolish prohibition had kept us from dancing with one another. As a musical person, I had always wanted to move my body whenever I heard music. However, because preachers decades ago convinced people to turn their discomfort about moving their own bodies into a religious dogma, I had never learned to dance.

Trish had heard this tirade more than once, so she decided to put an end to it. A few days after I opened her birthday gift, we made an appointment with a dance instructor.

In the first lesson, the teacher showed us how we could move our feet without stepping on one another. In our next lesson, we actually did a simple dance to an old folk melody. Our dance instructor said we were doing great.

I wasn't doing great though. While dancing with Trish, I had started feeling some emotions I couldn't label. I made it through the second session, but I quickly went to the car when we were finished. I asked Trish to drive home because I was holding back tears. I was embarrassed, but I couldn't seem to snap out of it. Something was wrong with me; I just didn't know what.

That was the day we began to realize that our marriage was in deep trouble. I knew that I wanted something more than I was getting from our relationship, but I had no idea what it was. I didn't even know how to tell Trish what I was feeling.

That experience was the beginning of an intense search for mental and emotional health—a search that would last for many years. Before we were through, we would attend couples' therapy, personal counseling, and 12-step groups. Finally, both of us would pursue graduate studies in psychology and postgraduate work in trauma, abuse, and deprivation.

(Believe me, that last paragraph covers more time, energy, and emotion than I could ever write in a single book.)

During those years, Trish and I continued to explore the issues that had kept us from experiencing intimacy. We discovered that though we had been business partners, parents, and even friends, we had never been lovers. Furthermore, we didn't know how.

For us, faith had been a matter of following rules and experiencing intense worship. We loved our children and tried to be good church leaders. We were faithful to one another, if one defines faithfulness as not having extramarital affairs. Most of the time, we treated each other politely.

We just didn't know how to be intimate. We couldn't dance.

We met talking about missionary work at a Bible college. After we were married, we plunged right into that work. Our "courtship" was platonic in nearly every sense of the word; we talked very little about erotic or even romantic life. We had decided to get married in order to serve the Lord. We wanted to save as many people as possible before the "great and terrible day of the Lord."

We connected sexually the best we knew how (after church work was done). We were poorly informed and clumsy. It wasn't very satisfying for either of us. I was often frustrated by our marriage's lack of erotic life, so I tried to pray my desire away. I figured that the battle for one's soul is intense; I decided to "defeat the devil" by plunging myself deeper into God's work. It's a common Christian cop-out.

The church, I discovered, like the culture at large, is usually willing to accommodate workaholism. That allowed me to find fulfillment in ministry and to avoid the emptiness at home.

The vacuum at the core of our marriage was just one of those things, I thought.

We made our marriage work until we accepted an appointment to a church that had been rocked by the moral indiscretions of its staff. As the years went by, our struggle to heal our church began to expose the poverty of our relationship. For the first time in my life, I began to think about establishing a new life and a new career. I then began to take concrete steps toward doing just that.

In the meantime, Trish was having her own epiphany. She too was realizing that we both needed some sort of breakthrough. Her apathy was turning to anger, and she began to face the fact that something had to change. As our children began to leave home, we became ever more aware of our lack of intimate relationship. Without children and church to connect us, we had no reason to stay together. Our future together looked dark.

We finally entered therapy. We signed up for a week of intensive work at Psychological Counseling Services in Scottsdale, Arizona.

I'll never forget the first evening of that week. After each of us had spent the day with various therapists, we met with three of them and discussed our treatment.

"Well," Dr. Earle said, "both of you claim, independently of one another, that you never fight."

I was proud when I heard Dr. Earle say that. So I laughed as I replied, "That's true, Dr. Earle. We rarely fuss about anything."

Now it was his time to laugh.

"We were amazed that you both thought that this lack of engagement was healthy," he said. "As a matter of fact, there's not enough energy in your marriage to fuss. Your marriage is in serious danger because both of you are so empty and angry. You aren't even willing to share that fact with one another."

We drove home in silence, fearing what would come next.

That week was filled with moments of truth in which we each told each other about how we had yearned for more than what our marriage seemed capable of giving. When the week ended, we knew only that the struggle ahead would be long and uncertain.

We were right.

We had committed ourselves to weekly sessions as a couple as well as individual sessions. As the months went by, we realized that we had rarely experienced intimacy at any level with one another. Indeed, we hardly knew how to acknowledge our own needs and desires even to ourselves.

The first thing we learned was how to get angry. We learned that when we were angry, we should say so. We discovered that we could get angry and even speak with intensity without insulting one another. We learned to freely express issues we had suppressed before.

Slowly, we learned to grow more intimate with one another intellectually, emotionally, and finally, even sexually. It was hard work, and it took a long time. We read and talked, we explored our religious and cultural background, and gradually our intellectual journey became an emotional connection.

Real physical intimacy was the most difficult part of our journey. That is sad and embarrassing for both of us, but it is the truth. That is why Trish and I both have such an interest in sexuality—we had difficulty with it for so long.

Many years after that moment on the dance floor, I experienced my most intimate moment with Trish. She had emerged from a coma caused by a brain aneurysm and had been transferred to rehab. There, she would learn how to walk and feed herself again. The hospital personnel told me that because she wouldn't have a roommate for three days, I was welcome to spend those nights with her.

I slept on a cot beside her bed. When I lay down, I held her hand. Naturally though, as I fell asleep, I let go. On one of those nights, I woke up hearing her trying to move. She was groping about in the darkness, searching for something. I realized that she was searching for my hand!

When I reached out and touched her hand, she sighed and then went back to sleep.

I lay there for a long time, just holding her hand. I knew that she wasn't yet fully aware of things. Nonetheless, she knew enough to want to touch me. It wasn't exactly a tango, it wasn't wild, unrestrained sex, but it was an intimate dance. Our bodies were touching, and through them, so were our souls.

What a journey we have had. Who would have thought that we would end up studying together, even doing a considerable amount of our studies in sex therapy! Besides all of that, we are really doing God's work together.

As we have continued to pastor a flock, we have been amazed to discover how many believers share our struggle with intimacy impairment. This has given us a place to connect deeply with others who hurt like we have.

RELATIONSHIPS FORM US

We are not islands, isolated from other people. As Aristotle so famously said, "We are social creatures." How we relate or fail to relate with others determines who we become.

We form our being, including our spiritual being, through social interaction. Our relationships slowly form our personality. As we learn (or fail to learn) from others, our being emerges.

Intimacy, the deepest level of social interaction, develops and reveals our hopes, fears, dreams, sorrows, and joys. That is why intimacy can be so terrifying and why we often run from it even though we so deeply desire it.

The Bible warns us that "it is a fearful thing to fall into the hands of the living God."[1] However, it is a fearful thing to fall into anyone's hands. When others have something we need, they have power over us. That is scary!

Relationships are also mirrors in which we see our authentic selves. We often discover in relationships (just as in mirrors) things we did not really want to learn. Intimacy, therefore, whether sexual or spiritual, is about nothing less than acknowledging the truth about who we really are, not only to ourselves but to our beloved.

In sexual intimacy, not only our body but our whole self gets naked!

The physical sensations of sex are certainly pleasurable, but most people long for more. Most people long for a mental and emotional connection that will allow their souls to see and to be seen, to hear and to be heard, and to feel and be felt.

Such intimacy requires trust and the ability to become emotionally naked. It also requires us to pay deep attention to the touch, movement, sounds, and scent of our lover. Intimate sex is the process of assessing what is really going on inside our partner. Otherwise, sex becomes a way of using a person to enhance our own fantasies. No true communication between sexual partners occurs when this happens. Each partner remains isolated and unconnected, hungering for intimacy but too terrified to give or to receive it. Without intimacy, both partners will feel like objects rather than like persons being invited into the deepest kind of human relationship.

This is why the Holy Scriptures often refer to people having sex as "knowing" one another. This euphemism suggests that sex is an act of seeing into another person. We long for this kind of knowing, both with God and with a human partner.

The Bible also assumes that the body is the means through which this kind of knowing takes place.

BECOMING COMFORTABLE WITH OUR BODIES

Blair McKinsey was a 30-year-old woman who had gone to therapy because she seemed to freeze every time her husband wanted sex.

"The funny thing about it," she said to Dr. Andréa, "I sometimes feel aroused during the day. I'll be thinking that having sex that night will be nice. Then he'll come home and I'll start flirting, sending out all the right signals and all. But when he does stuff like lighting candles and turning on music…well, I just start getting anxious and angry.

"The other night, I heard him getting the bedroom ready, and I began to fret; I really got mad when I heard the music. So on an impulse, I suddenly put on this 'old woman' robe that he hates and walked into the bedroom fuming. Boy, did that pour the cold water on things! He was hurt and frustrated and just left the room. Everything between us turned sour for days."

"What about sex do you dislike the most?" Dr. Andréa asked.

"Being naked!" Blair said quickly. "He looks at every part of me so intently. I don't even look at myself that way."

"Oh?" Dr. Andréa interjected. "When and under what conditions are you ever naked?"

"Hmm…well, I take a shower naked of course, and when I change clothes; just the normal times when most people are naked."

"Are you ever naked for any length of time, such as when you are alone in the house?"

"No, I'd be afraid that someone would come to the house or something. I'm just not comfortable when I'm not wearing clothes."

"Blair, you'll never be likely to learn to be comfortable with Bill when you're naked if you never become comfortable that way when you are alone. Would you be willing to schedule three times this week to be alone at your house? Would you be willing to walk around your house without any clothes for an hour or so?"

"Okay…but what will I be doing all that time?"

"Anything you like. Watch TV, read a book or magazine, whatever. Just notice the sensation of everything that touches your skin. Your skin is the largest organ of your body, and it's filled with sensation, so pay attention to it! Also, look at yourself in the mirror. Try to look at yourself with wonder, the way your husband does. Don't dwell on any flaws you think you may have—I guarantee you that your husband's not doing that! Do that three times this week and write down what you feel when you are naked. We'll talk about what you write in our next session," Dr. Andréa concluded.

Dr. Andréa gave good advice. Though Blair may have other sexual issues that did not emerge in her season with Dr. Andréa, we already know that she is uncomfortable with her body. (She is not, in other words, intimate with herself.) She is not likely to feel free to express herself sexually with her husband until she finds a way to deal with that discomfort.

Sexual issues are almost always life issues. Sex is just the place they show up because that is where we feel most exposed. Sex uncovers our core character traits. The more intense sex becomes, the more we expose our being.

This is one reason why it is not a good idea to have sex with someone before we become intimate with them in other ways. People who become sexual with one another too early in a relationship, before they touch one another at other levels, will usually find that sexualizing the relationship subverts the process of becoming truly intimate.

Christians, of course, believe that one should not have sex with another person outside marriage. However, believers often also expect their sex lives to be wonderful in marriage just because they have "kept the rules" before the wedding. It almost never happens that way. Believers, like anyone else, will probably be disappointed with their sex lives if they don't become intimate in other ways before marriage. Furthermore, if believers don't feel sexual hunger for one another before they consummate their union, they are not likely to have satisfying sex on the honeymoon. Water has to get hot before it boils!

In the past few years, I have heard Evangelical youth pastors teach that believers shouldn't date before marriage. Their aim is to discourage promiscuity and the sort of "horse trading" approach to relationships that can destroy a spiritual community. I understand that. However, I think this approach does a lot of damage in the long run. Both as a pastor and a therapist, I know what happens when an individual bases his or her choice for a spouse solely upon some sort of inner sense that

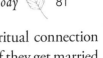

"this is the one." Individuals can share a deep spiritual connection without sharing other important common ground. If they get married only because they share spiritual beliefs and experiences, their resulting relationship may not be strong enough to sustain their union.

Spiritual unity is vital, but it is not the only component of a healthy marriage. If one spouse wants children and the other does not, if one enjoys sex and the other does not, if one pursues intellectual life and the other disdains it...disconnections like these are not trivial. They do not disappear simply because two people share spiritual life. That's why the idea of not dating before marriage seems so preposterous to me. People need ways to become appropriately intimate before selecting a permanent mate.

Intimacy is about telling the truth. It resists the natural tendency to avoid unpleasant differences in order to sell one's self to another.

Someone once defined intimacy as "in to me, you see." When our relationships go beyond the polite acquaintance stage, we begin to emotionally disrobe in the other persons' presence. We stop being coy around them about our deepest beliefs, ambitions, fears, tastes, cultural preferences, and so forth. Our authentic being emerges from behind the facades that we employ in more superficial relationships. If we insist on keeping the facade when friends or our spouse is ready to go deeper, they will sooner or later withdraw their invitation to us for intimate connection; they may even go away.

INTIMACY WITH GOD

Amazingly, many of us seem to believe intimacy is about being nice and sweet all the time. It is nothing of the sort!

In the book of Genesis, God makes plans to destroy the wicked city of Sodom. Before He carries out His intention, however, He decides to share His idea with His friend Abraham. So He gets Abraham aside and shares with him what He plans to do. Here's a paraphrase of their conversation:

"What?" Abraham asks. "Do you really plan to destroy everyone? What if you destroy righteous people along with the wicked? What if you find fifty righteous people in that city? Would you still destroy the entire town?"

"No," God answers. "I won't destroy the city if I can find fifty righteous people."

"Okay," Abraham replies. "What about forty? That's just ten less. Would you destroy the city over just ten people less than your quota of fifty righteous people?"

"No," God says, "Forty righteous people will be enough to keep me from destroying the city."

The argument continues as Abraham intercedes for the lives of the people of Sodom. At one point, Abraham shouts out in desperation, "Shall not the Judge of all the earth do right?"

When I read that sentence, I want to step back. It feels as if someone is going to get hurt. God, however, gives His reasons and allows His friend to keep arguing. Why? Because God wants His friends to tell Him the truth. He wants us to say what is really going on inside us.

That is intimacy.

When I was going through therapy, my counselors were really hammering at me about disclosing my true feelings. During that time, I made a spiritual discovery: All of the heroes of the Bible had doubts about their faith and stated those doubts in prayer. The psalms, which show us how to pray, are not all sweet and nice. Some of them say things like this: "I cry out to you day and night, and You seem not to take notice. I'm in despair because You aren't answering me." Job, whose friends keep giving good advice about "getting right with God," answers them with some of the most impious language in the Bible. However, when God shows up at the end of the book, He declares Job to be His friend.

Intimacy, in marriage and in friendship, is about being truthful. This doesn't mean we shouldn't choose our words carefully or that we should throw courtesy out the window—we can be honest and still protect other people's dignity. But we can't be intimate if we are too afraid to tell people what we feel.

Intimacy also involves common symbols, like wedding bands,

special foods, and pieces of music that remind individuals of their bonds with others. Lovers may get misty-eyed when hearing a certain song. They may, like Trish and me, make a pot of tea to sip during important discussions. Such habits and symbols create an atmosphere of shared reality and intimate space that nurtures and reaffirms the bond between friends or lovers.

When we become intimate with someone, the resulting friendship acquires certain habits and material props. We have coffee together, read and discuss books together, go to favorite places together, and so forth. In other words, we develop anchors to symbolize and embody the relationship.

For more than 20 years, Trish and I have been friends with John and Barbara and with Ron and Charlotte. We have been such close friends that people naturally assume we have a lot in common. Actually, we don't. What we share is a love of books and a deep interest in spiritual matters. We differ politically, aesthetically, and to some extent, even in the way we express our faith. However, we share a love for good coffee, well-written books, rhythm and blues, finely prepared food, and the Rocky Mountains.

We also live in different places, so meetings are mostly by e-mail and phone. We stay connected by recommending books to one another, which we read and make a part of our ongoing discussion. We support one another in the momentous occasions of life: We have been present for one another's ordinations, when our marriages have been in difficulty, when our loved ones have been ill, and so forth.

I have enjoyed a friendship with Allan for many years as well. Our connection is based on books and theology. We grew up in the same denomination and supported one another when we left it. Since then, we have talked on the phone, written e-mails, and exchanged books. We debate his persistent and pernicious Calvinism and my postmodern tendencies. As I write this book, I see an icon that he sent to Trish and me when we built a home in Phoenix. I look at the icon, and I know that our friendship is an important part of my life.

All friendships involve meeting places and symbolic connections because symbols and locations anchor relationships and help form their character. Our relationship with God is no exception. It too involves symbolic connectors.

In the Bible, God set up a yearly meeting with his Old Testament people around a special meal called Passover. In the New Testament, He set up another meeting around a meal we call Communion, or Eucharist. Thus, food can serve as an anchor for our fellowship with God. These special meals are not magic, and they cannot create the relationship if it doesn't exist otherwise. However, if we do have a relationship with God, a meeting with Him and with fellow believers around His table can be very intimate indeed.

In Communion, we pray special prayers together—often the Lord's Prayer. We confess our sins. We greet one another in the passing of the peace. Usually, we sing songs that are meaningful to our particular spiritual community. In these and other ways, we gradually prepare ourselves for the moment in which we will eat the bread and drink the wine. When we leave the service and return to our everyday life, we feel that we have somehow touched the source of our faith and life. We go back into the world renewed by our relationship with God and His people.

We can meet God around His Book. However, this requires effort on our part.

When my friend Barbara attended her husband's family reunion for the first time, she thought they were going to fight. John's family had started debating some passage in the Bible, and each person was passionately supporting his or her position with Scripture.

"Their voices got louder and louder," Barbara says. "I was terrified. I thought they were going to fight! Then Grandma suddenly called from the kitchen to say that dinner was ready, and it was all over! I was a wreck, but they were acting like nothing had happened."

Barbara had described a family whose intellectual life revolves around the Bible. Its family members had familiarized themselves with its stories and ideas and enjoyed examining and debating what they meant. Their emotional intensity was not anger; it was passion and intimacy.

Some years ago, I saw a painting that I wish I had purchased. In it, a group of rabbis are passionately arguing. One holds a book and is pointing to it. Another is red-faced and obviously displeased. The third rabbi strokes his beard and seems to be considering what the other two are saying. The scene embodies the spirit of rabbinical dialogue about Scripture. They debate because the words matter to them. They are passionate about the Book because through the Book they touch the face of God.

This kind of passionate engagement with a text can bring heartache and division, no doubt about it. However, it is also a kind of intimacy. No one invests energy in a book he cares nothing about. When one cares about the Book of books, he learns what it says. He examines what it means. As he does, he will encounter its Author.

A FINAL WORD ABOUT INTIMACY

As I said, Trish and I have learned to argue. We even practice from time to time so we won't get rusty! We have learned that when we are not afraid to argue passionately, we can sometimes do other things passionately!

We still don't dance, if "dance" must mean "purposeful and artistic movement to music." I still believe that not dancing was a loss. So I still resent the well-intentioned but silly teaching that crippled us unnecessarily in that way. However, we have learned to dance in more significant ways.

Trish nearly died and had a long, hard road to recovery. We experienced things in that season of life that are too intimate to write about. Many of them were unpleasant. However, we promised long ago that we would share life together "in sickness and in health, for richer and for poorer." It is a promise that we have kept.

By keeping that promise, we have discovered steps for our own unique dance. Though our steps may not always appear graceful to others, they are, nonetheless, our steps. We take them together, all the way home.

Six

GROANINGS THAT CANNOT BE UTTERED

WHEN INTIMACY GOES BEYOND WORDS

One of my granddaughters can't talk yet, but she gets excited and giggles when she sees me. She also makes cute noises that I try to repeat.

We can't have a conversation about literary criticism or politics (yet!), but we do seem to understand one another. (Every grandparent will understand what I'm saying!)

Can we call what my granddaughter and I are saying to one another a language? That's difficult to say. It is certainly communication! Whether it is a language depends on your definition of language. Sometimes the deepest communication we can have with another person is literally too much for words.

That's what St. Paul is getting at in Romans when he says, "We do not know what we should pray for as we ought, but the Spirit Himself makes intercession for us with groanings which cannot be uttered."[1]

I've always thought of this passage as a rather tortured phrase. If a groaning can't be uttered, how does one hear the sound? Despite its awkwardness though, Paul's strange choice of words points to a phenomenon familiar to most of us, at least in some context. People often communicate meaning through sounds that can't be found in any dictionary. We know, after all, when a groan means "I'm suffering," or "I'm bored," or "I'm aroused." We know when a sigh means, "I'm content" and when it means, "I'm exhausted!" Human beings often make sounds that express meaning but that are not really words. They are probably expressions from the right hemisphere of our brain, from where we process emotion, metaphor, art, and the like. Whatever they are, we use them!

St. Paul is saying that we may make such sounds during intense prayer, and that their meaning is private rather than public. We make those sounds in prayer when we are experiencing overwhelming emotions such as awe, fear, grief, or joy.

And why not? They are some of the first sounds we make when we are learning to communicate. They are connected to the deepest parts of our emotional lives. Why wouldn't intense prayer employ these primal sounds? After all, I use them to talk to my granddaughter. If I ever win the lottery (because I happen to pick up a ticket someone dropped on the sidewalk, of course), I will probably express my surprise with sounds one cannot find in a dictionary.

Then there's that other place where this sort of communication occurs—when we have sex.

That makes me think about a joke I heard years ago in my high school locker room (which is, of course, always a good place to pick up sexual information!): One morning, Billy Bob tells his friend Jim Bob that he didn't get any sleep the night before. "The lady in the apartment next to mine kept yelling for someone to bring her a candy bar."

"What do you mean?" Jim Bob wants to know.

"Well," Billy Bob replies, "all night long she just kept yelling, 'Oh Henry! Oh Henry!' "

(A friend told me that when I use this joke, I need to explain to new generations that Oh Henry! is a candy bar!)

Obviously, Billy Bob misunderstood his neighbor's intentions. But Henry (whoever he was) understood perfectly!

The language of lovers is a specialized and private one; it often makes little sense to these who overhear it.

We use primal sounds in sex because when sex gets really intense, words are simply inadequate to express what we are feeling. In fact, the entire sexual experience can be thought of as a form of language for which the primal sounds serve as punctuation.

SEX AS LANGUAGE

If we are to think of sex as language, we need to think about what language is.

Language is a shared system of symbols that serves as an interface between minds. It is how minds use the actions of physical bodies to exchange information with one another.

The symbols that make up a language can be almost anything—motions of a hand, sounds from a mouth, marks on a piece of paper, or even puffs of smoke. To use anything as a language, all we have to do is agree with someone that a sound, an action, or a thing will stand for something else. Three puffs of smoke in quick succession will stand for "danger," for example. Showing the middle finger of one's hand while keeping the other fingers folded will mean "terrible insult." The more people who agree to use the same symbols, the more we begin to recognize their shared symbols as a language.

Computers talk to one another by agreeing that "1" means "current on" and "0" means "current off." Computer chips are switching devices that turn electric current on and off millions of times a second. That allows the computers to process what is essentially an alphabet, consisting of two symbols—"1" and "0." To my computer, this sentence is a series of ones and zeros that would fill several pages of print. All computer programs depend on that simple agreement, called the binary system. It makes modern commerce and communication possible.

Like the binary system, all language is a series of agreements about how to use common symbols. We use those symbols to construct conversation.

Furthermore, people must have a common language in order to share their ideas. A Frenchman has a difficult time talking to a person from India who speaks Urdu. A deaf man can't get his thoughts across to a hearing man by using sign language if the hearing man cannot understand the gestures.

In fact, for conversation to have much depth, we must continually refine our languages. That's why we study grammar or expand our vocabulary. Language is constantly evolving; it requires our constant attention. Whether a language is spoken, signed, or acted out, we must deliberately work to acquire and consciously refine it in order to use it to express our thoughts and emotions.

In a way of speaking, sex is a language. It uses touch, scent, sound, and movement to communicate with one's self and with one's partner. When people have sex, they may communicate tenderness, loneliness, fear, affection, or even apathy. They will always communicate something. Furthermore, at some level, their partner always understands the message they communicate sexually.

Of course, sex is a special sort of conversation. We hope it is not two simultaneous monologues! Adults should become fluent enough in the art of sexual communication that their emotions, desires, and delight become obvious to their partners. That way, sexual partners learn to share a profound unity. That is what makes sex an intimate conversation.

As with any other kind of conversation, the quality of sexual intercourse depends on the knowledge and trust of those who are communicating. Sex can be a simple matter of giving one or both partners relief from sexual tension. Most people can do this for themselves or for a partner without much training. However, sex can also be a delectable excursion through hours of fun and games, poetry and romance, teasing and experimenting with physical pleasure. That's what books like the Song of Solomon and the Kama Sutra encourage.

For most couples, lovemaking is something between the two extremes of a "quickie" and an erotic vacation. However, if a couple desires more than a "fast roll in the sack" before sleep, they have to intentionally develop their ability to speak and comprehend the language of sex. Sex at this level simply does not come naturally; we must intentionally acquire it.

OUR MOTHER TONGUE

We often affectionately refer to the spoken language of our childhood as "our mother tongue." Even if we speak many languages, we usually prefer our first language when addressing matters of the heart.

The truth is, our real mother tongue is not a spoken language at all. Our real mother tongue consists of the movements we make with our bodies (particularly our faces) to express our deepest emotions. We sometimes call this "body language." Counselors, however, call it "affect" (pronounced by emphasizing the first letter of the word.)

The word "affect" derives from the Latin *affectus,* which literally means "acted upon." We call body language "affect" because our unconscious mind acts upon thousands of tiny muscles in our face and other parts of our bodies to reveal what we are feeling.

We could think of our unconscious mind as something like a conductor that constantly directs an emotional symphony. The muscles in our face are like the individual players in the orchestra; they each play their part as the conductor directs from the score. As the various instruments weave their notes together, melodies, harmonies, and rhythms emerge to create and convey an experience that is filled with emotion.

Body language is difficult to hide or to fabricate. The pieces of information that play out on our face and other parts of our bodies bubble up from the deepest parts of self. Thus, they reveal our true emotions and attitudes in each moment. In fact, they are usually a more accurate witness of our inner self than what we want to reveal to others or sometimes even to ourselves.

WHAT WERE THEY THINKING?

An experiment a few years ago illustrated how out of touch we can be about our own body language. In the experiment, a university psychology department outfitted volunteers with various kinds of sensors to record states of excitement and arousal. The volunteers were then asked to watch pornographic material. As they did, the researchers stopped from time to time to ask them what they were feeling about the material.

Some of the volunteers admitted they found the material arousing. Others claimed to be unaffected by it. Still others were angry and warned that they intended to do everything they could to strengthen their community's antiobscenity laws.

The sensors, however, revealed that all of the men and the women had unmistakable genital arousal. Also, everyone's eyes dilated; everyone's pulse raced. As the experiment continued, the researchers discovered something interesting: Neither those who claimed to be bored nor those who were angry were lying. Lie detector testing revealed that they believed they were being truthful about their response to the porn.

The researchers finally concluded that the reason for the discrepancy was this: Although arousal reveals itself similarly in everyone (at least physiologically speaking), the way individuals register and interpret their own arousal differs considerably from culture to culture and from person to person.

If one has a racing pulse because he is sexually aroused, but he has not learned to associate a racing pulse with sexual desire, he may well associate it with fear or anger. This implies that though our unconscious mind is constantly communicating through our body, we must learn how to pay attention and how to interpret what it is saying. This is especially true of experiences that are new to us.

Sexual arousal is instinctual, but we don't always recognize or process it as arousal. People who grow up in an environment where sex is feared, dreaded, or ignored can experience their own arousal as danger.

How many old comedies depict some character nervously wiping his brow as he stares at a woman in a skimpy outfit? We laugh when he keeps complaining about the heat in the room because we know that his sweat is not really about room temperature! He is defining arousal in perhaps the only way he can. As we observe him, we know that he is unaware of some important information about himself.

The movie *Pleasantville* was not exactly a blockbuster, but it was brilliantly written and produced. As we watch the people of Pleasantville cling to their facade of innocence, we both envy and pity them. We realize that their innocence is due to their lack of basic adult knowledge, especially in sexual matters. When Mary Sue, the visitor from our world to Pleasantville, begins to kiss her boyfriend, he suddenly looks terrified, stares at his lap and says, "I'm sick! Something is wrong with me. What's happening?"

Mary Sue, who knows a little more about such things, smiles and says, "What is happening is what is supposed to happen. It's a good thing. You'll see!"

Pleasantville is a movie about how people who remain unaware of their own desires miss out on life. We may not agree with the way the people of *Pleasantville* respond to their awakening desires, but we must agree with the movie's premise that they should respond. Otherwise, they are not even fully human.

Sylvan Tomkins was a scientist who did extensive research on body language. He came to believe that adult emotions are learned, not instinctual. Infants and children develop them by gradually refining a few basic instinctual responses into the subtleties of what we think of as human emotion. For example, fear is an instinct. Cautious apprehension, however, is a refined perception and interpretation of one's own fear. Becoming aware that one's apprehension is due to a bad past experience is an even more developed emotion. Tomkins learned that people can develop a wide range of emotional perceptions, which they use to comprehend their own self and to respond appropriately.

Tomkins also discovered that people first learn to read their own body language as a way to figure out what is going on inside themselves.[2] He saw that people need to learn how to understand their own emotions before they can understand the emotions of others.

HOW WE LEARN OUR MOTHER TONGUE

Mothers talk to their babies differently than they talk to adults. In fact, a mother first connects to her infant through the warmth of her embrace. Her baby quickly learns to respond to her with coos and sighs and with frustrated grunts and grimaces. For several months, this nonverbal language proves astonishingly capable of revealing the child's will and emotions.

Mothers understand this language. Indeed, we all do. That is why I call it our "mother tongue."

As a child gradually masters his family's spoken language, he begins to think in words. The child becomes a conscious being. In time, he nearly forgets his first language of human interaction, the language that created the powerful bond he shared with his mother.

SEX AND THE RECOVERY OF OUR FIRST LANGUAGE

A spoken language is the foundation of human community. However, words often prove inadequate for our most intimate experiences. This is especially true of sex. To communicate sexual arousal and desire, we return to the natural language of the unconscious. We use touch and primal sounds to express our deepest feelings. Sexual communication is severely crippled when we try to rely on our spoken language alone.

Good sex takes us to places where we speak another language, the language of erotic life.

Learning to release our instinctual sounds and movement frees us to communicate with our partner at deep levels. However, we can sometimes be as surprised as our partner about what emerges from inside us. As Sylvan Tomkins discovered, affect is as much about communication between one's own conscious and unconscious self as it is about communicating with others!

Tomkins discovered this while working with cats.[3] He had already determined that a cat purrs when we pet it because of a primitive instinct. He found this discovery unsatisfying, however. You stroke a cat and it purrs, but why? We know that the cat is happy with what it is feeling, but what difference would that make in the wild, where historically most cats have lived? The more he studied and researched, the more convinced he became that the biological purpose for the purr was to amplify the cat's awareness of its own pleasure. He discovered that when he played a recording of a purr to another cat, its brain registered pleasure and interest.

The implication for human sexual experience is probably obvious: Sexual sounds not only communicate to our partner what we are feeling but also amplify our own pleasure. People sigh, moan, and move around during sex because this rewards their partner but also because it enhances their own perception of the experience.

When sexual communication is uninhibited, it becomes an intense bond between the partners. We could almost say that the lovers' brains and nervous systems become interfaced. Each partner becomes, at least for a short time and in a limited way, an extension of the emotions and pleasure of the other. This experience makes one feel as though her soul is touching that of her partner.

For sex to become more than a mere scratching of a physical itch, partners must learn how not to suppress their instinctual movements and sounds. This intimate and soulful language helps make sex an "intercourse," not only between the lovers' physical bodies but also between their minds, emotions, and spirits. Sometimes, this makes sex a veritable interpenetration of souls.

PRAYER AND INTIMACY

The God described in Hebrew Scripture is a Spirit who seeks to be heard and to be known. The prophets claim that God is, in fact, constantly speaking and that to hear Him, we must learn how to listen. Thus, the first word of the great Hebrew prayer—"Hear O Israel, the LORD our God, the LORD is one"—is *shma,* or "listen."

Thus, when the ancient Hebrews teach us to pray, they do not begin by teaching us to speak. They begin by teaching us to listen.

Something is quite startling about beginning our prayer with the word "listen." The word cannot be, after all, an instruction to God! It has to be an instruction to our own inner self.

Shma is a plea to our own soul. "Open up to a new way! Get unstuck! Come out from behind your defended perspective! Dare to venture out from your comfortable isolation!"

Shma is an invitation to enter into conversation with a Being who is very different from us. He is holy, or other.

In sex, we communicate first to our partner but also to ourselves. In prayer, we reveal the state of our soul first to God but also to ourselves.

We can pray in order to do our duty (we may think, *God will get really ticked if I don't say my prayers*). We can pray in order to experience release (many of the psalms lend themselves to this need). Or we can pray in order to converse with God.

Like sex, as prayer becomes ever more intimate, it seeks to become embodied. We begin expressing prayer physically by doing things such as raising our hands, closing our eyes, kneeling, or making the sign of the cross. In other words, prayer gradually becomes sacramental—our spiritual experience begins manifesting itself through human gestures.

For many Christians, the celebration of Holy Communion is an opportunity to use motion, speech, and food as manifestations of deep, soulful prayer. It is a way for Christians to use their bodies in order to open up their souls.

Christians may also use the primal sounds of their unconscious in their most intimate spiritual moments, as they have been doing since the earliest days of their Christian faith. That is what St. Paul was talking about when he said the Spirit prays for us with groans and inarticulate sounds. The writer of the book of Hebrews claims that Christ prayed this way too when He offered up prayers and supplications with vehement cries and tears. And He was heard.[4]

This comment in the book of Hebrews is an interesting reflection on how Christ prayed because the Gospel accounts do not reveal this side of the Lord's prayer life (with the exception of His prayers at Lazarus' tomb and in Gethsemane).

Public Hebrew prayer primarily involved the recitation of Scripture, usually the psalms. Both Jesus and Paul followed this Hebrew practice, and historically Christians have done the same through what we call "common prayers." Even in death, Christ recited a psalm He probably memorized as a child. However, He evidently had another side to His prayer life, a more primal, less rational side.

Public Hebrew prayer traditionally followed a pattern of revelation, reflection, and response. Because God had spoken to His people through the Scriptures, believers were to reflect on them. Then they were to respond to the Scriptures through silent meditation and, even more importantly, through their audible recitation of the words of God. This, for the Hebrew, was prayer: speaking God's thoughts back to God.

However, another kind of prayer could take spiritual intimacy to another level. A believer could offer to God his or her unedited and unrehearsed thoughts, feelings, physical movements, and sometimes, even unintelligible sounds of anguish or joy.

In other words, intimate prayer could employ the language of primal sounds and gestures. This was an intimate and private form of prayer. It is the language of lovers. It is neither intended nor usually appropriate for public. St. Paul makes this clear.

> If I pray in a tongue, my spirit prays, but my understanding is unfruitful. What is the conclusion then? I will pray with the spirit, and I will also pray with the understanding. I will sing with the spirit, and I will also sing with the understanding. Otherwise, if you bless with the spirit, how will he who occupies the place of the uninformed say "Amen" at your giving of thanks, since he does not understand what you say? For you indeed give thanks well, but the other is not edified.
>
> I thank my God I speak with tongues more than you all; yet in the church I would rather speak five words with my

understanding, that I may teach others also, than ten thousand words in a tongue.[5]

As we have seen earlier, for the Hebrews, "soul" referred to everything that is involved with being human. Clearly then, Hebrew prayer was not meant to be abstract, passionless, or ghostly. For an ancient Hebrew, spirituality could not be a flight from the body or an escape from the material world. Hebrew spirituality was earthy, rooted in life, connected with physical movement. It was sometimes intellectually sophisticated, but at other times it was simply a primitive cry from the depths of one's soul. Therefore a psalm can express lofty sentiments in beautifully crafted words, or a prophet can wail and thrash his body about, or a publican can simply beat his breast, saying, "God, have mercy."

Prayer involves all these things because they are all parts of what it means to be human.

This is what we offer to a lover and especially to the lover of our souls: all that we are, all that we feel, and all that we think—unedited, unrehearsed, and unpolished. There are times for formality, such as when we eat at a banquet dressed in our finest. There, we recite carefully crafted words. There are also times when we sigh and moan because we feel something beyond what our spoken language is able to express.

In the same way, a praying person learns to express all of her unedited feelings and thoughts to God, to pray with the spirit and not only with the understanding. In the process of speaking to God, prayer becomes the soul's mirror, a way of knowing her own self.

Perhaps we should say that prayer *can* become the soul's mirror. Unfortunately, we can use prayer, just as we can use sex, as a way to *disconnect* from others and even from ourselves. Whether prayer or sex becomes a connection or an escape depends on whether we use them to communicate or as a means of escape from life and reality. When we use sex or prayer to connect with another, paradoxically, we often discover ourselves.

When we have spent our lives hiding from ourselves, we should not be surprised that we have such limited means to connect to others. Therefore, often the first experience people have of themselves as an authentic and vibrant being is at a moment of intense intimacy with another person. Such an experience can give us the courage to cast aside the self-censorship that edits our thoughts and feelings before others can experience them. Suddenly, we find ourselves wailing or laughing, dancing or weeping because our soul has finally found a way to be heard through "groanings which cannot be uttered."

Seven

I'm Beside Myself!

THE ROLE OF ECSTASY IN
SEXUAL AND SPIRITUAL LIFE

I was in the Ukraine, taking Bibles to believers just a few years before the collapse of the Soviet regime. One night, as I was sitting in a restaurant, a man sat down in one of the empty chairs at my table and blurted out a question.

"Do you give Bibles to Jews?"

"What?" I replied, with a puzzled look.

"Jews. We are Jews. We also do not have Holy Scriptures. Can you give us Bibles?"

"Well, sure," I said. "However, my Bible contains the New Testament."

"Not to worry," he said. "Me and my friends—we have never read the Holy Scriptures. Our rabbi does not even have a Bible."

Delighted to help, I went up to my hotel room and brought down 15 Bibles. When I returned, my table was surrounded with young adults who took the Bibles and then hugged me, one by one.

"Now we will do something for you," my Jewish friend said.

At that, they pushed the tables back, formed a circle, and began to clap. Suddenly, a young lady whom I would have never thought of as beautiful entered the circle. She then began to dance. Soon, she was twirling with all her might, moving her body in ways that were never sensual but that seemed to send bursts of energy out into the room. I couldn't keep my eyes off her face. She looked like an angel. She was caught up in a joy that was delightful and contagious, and I was mesmerized.

I have never forgotten her.

My Jewish friend was right. The dance was a gift. Since that moment, I have known what the Scripture means when it instructs us to "praise Him with the timbrel and dance."[1]

I'm amazed by the Western church's resistance to dance. Centuries of custom have nearly lobotomized us, eliminating all but the most carefully orchestrated response to what we claim is the hope of the world.

Culture also conditions us to resist ecstatic moments. It teaches us to remain in control because a plunge into joy is an abandonment of reason. We have learned not to twirl. Our faces seldom glow.

We do our duty. We follow the script. We stay in charge. What a pitiful waste of our potential for joy!

"Twirling" looks different for each of us because different personalities express themselves in different ways. God made us all to dance. He made us for passion. He made us not merely to exist but to have life more abundantly.

ECSTATIC EXPERIENCE

The word *exstasis* is Greek for "standing outside (oneself)." It expresses the experience of the self viewing the self as another. Therefore, the word *exstasis* is often translated "trance." Paul experienced it once in the temple, and Peter experienced it on the housetop as God prepared him to accept Gentiles into the church.[2]

Trance is focused attention upon an idea, a person, or an object that is either within one's imagination or out in the objective world. While in trance, one's perception of the objective or outside world becomes diminished. One's focus moves to the subjective world, the world within.

The Ukrainian Jewish dancer was entranced by her focused attention on movement. The outside world disappeared. She became her dance.

THE PHYSICAL DYNAMICS OF TRANCE

The brain manages our bodily functions through two major systems: the voluntary and involuntary systems. The *parasympathetic* nervous system governs those physical functions of which we are aware and that we can deliberately affect. Those of which we are normally unaware and that are usually beyond our conscious ability to affect are governed by the involuntary nervous system.

To write this sentence, I deliberately move my fingers across the computer keys, a function of my voluntary nervous system. However, I am not fully aware that my brain is also directing my heart and my lungs. I am unaware of those activities because they belong to the realm of the involuntary nervous system.

The two systems work together. Defining where one ends and the other begins is sometimes difficult. We can learn to become aware of our involuntary nervous system—such as heartbeat and breathing—and even learn how to exercise a degree of conscious control over these functions. Eastern cultures have developed disciplines to do such things, and from time to time we read of an experiment in which some guru meditates until his heartbeat is nearly imperceptible.

More importantly for our discussion, we can turn a complicated activity that requires conscious effort into one that does not. We do this by practicing the steps of the activity until it slowly becomes a process that our involuntary nervous system can manage. After we do this, we no longer need to pay so much attention to the activity. We become free to enjoy it as it automatically performs itself.

For example, someone can practice the basic steps of an athletic skill such as swimming until it gets encoded in her unconscious. What was at first a task gradually becomes a fluid and artful pleasure. The swimmer now moves gracefully through the water without conscious thought, no longer focusing her awareness on the strokes but rather on the sensual delight of the experience.

That's a convoluted way of saying that the swimmer is having fun!

People who have fun doing complicated things have worked hard to turn something that once required intense focus into an activity that no longer does. I was delighted by the seemingly effortless moves of the Ukrainian Jewish dancer, but I never saw her endless hours of practice that made her artful performance possible. Dance is a series of movements that one's body can memorize through repetition. After they are memorized, the movement becomes fluid and appears to be effortless and unrehearsed.

This is true also for the "sexual trance," in which sex becomes something more like a beautiful dance than like an anxious struggle.

Good sex requires knowledge. It also requires that the knowledge be accessed with little conscious effort. We have to learn to let go, allowing sex to flow from our involuntary system rather than from our voluntary system. Otherwise we either feel too incompetent or too uptight to enjoy it.

EMOTIONAL HEALING AND THE SHIFT OF CONSCIOUSNESS

Betty was exasperated with me.

"After seeing you these three weeks, I feel worse than I did before!" she said.

"I'm not surprised you feel that way," I replied. "However, we really are getting somewhere. You entered counseling because you realized that something you were doing or thinking wasn't working for you. You didn't know what that something was. You were *unconsciously incompetent*."

"What in the world does that mean?" she asked.

"It means you didn't know what you were doing to diminish your sense of life. As you have become aware of the things you've been doing that have hurt you and those you love, you have naturally felt a lot of shame and regret. Another way to describe what you are going through is that you have become *consciously incompetent.*"

"And that's progress?" she demanded.

"Sure. When you become aware of your incompetent thoughts or actions, you are no longer able to operate automatically. They become accessible for us to evaluate and to change."

"So I'm still going to be incompetent—I'll just be aware that I'm incompetent?" she asked sadly.

"Not at all," I quickly replied. "Our first goal was to make your incompetence conscious, so you wouldn't automatically keep doing hurtful things. Our next goal was to help you learn how to deliberately choose how you wanted to respond to life. If you keep working at it, you will begin to experience times when you become unconsciously competent, making good choices without a lot of effort."

"And that means I'll automatically act and think in a more healthy way than I do now, most of the time?" she asked.

"Exactly!" I said. "Unconscious competence is the best kind. Good choices flow out of who you are. They feel less contrived and forced. They feel like you!"

We function best in any area of life when a situation is challenging enough to be interesting and routine enough to be comfortable. For example, if we find a book too difficult, we tend to lose interest in it. However, if it is too elementary, we also tend to put it down. We usually enjoy reading books that both stretch us a little and that reward us with some immediate pleasure. We need the comfort of familiar things, and we also need novelty and variety. This is true for all areas of life, including sex.

We usually experience a deep sense of joy when we perform a complex skill that we have memorized and mastered. This is especially true when we are able to add some novel element to the performance that heightens our interest in it. For example, a musician who masters a piece and enjoys playing it without thought will experience even greater pleasure by adding some element of complexity that reawakens his personal interest and delight. When that happens, the piece becomes both old and new and thus reawakens his attention.

Complicated skills that we learn to do effortlessly can induce trance of the good sort—the kind that allows us to perform from deep within our being. Paradoxically, when someone has mastered a skill and allows it to flow effortlessly, he becomes free to focus attention on other elements of the performance, such as an audience.

Every actor or speaker knows that once she becomes comfortable with the content and delivery of a performance, she can read the crowd's reactions much more easily. That allows the performer to make small adjustments that allow her to connect even deeper to her audience.

Athletes and musicians often refer to this sense of connected performance as being "in the zone." It is a deeply pleasurable and rewarding experience. Fortunately, it is available to anyone who is willing to keep mastering new skills and releasing conscious control of those skills.

Sex is one of those activities that can be learned, practiced, performed, and experienced. It just takes intention, willingness to learn, and willingness to release oneself to the moment.

SEXUAL TRANCE

In enjoyable sex, a person's emotions and actions flow effortlessly from inside, allowing him to express intimacy and joy. It also allows him to focus consciously on his own sensations and on his partner's needs. He is no longer focused consciously on performance. When both partners are "in the zone," communication flows between them at such deep levels that they can feel as though they have gone "wireless." It is almost a sensation of being "interfaced." Admittedly, this is not an everyday occurrence. However, many couples have experienced it, and most who have not find it appealing.

Sexual trance is the result of becoming so focused on one another that time and environment fade. The partners experience such a unity that movement, sound, touch, and scent nearly consume their entire attention. Motion becomes fluid rather than contrived. Sex becomes soulful and deeply expressive. Calendars and clocks lose their value, and the partners become their own universe. It is a dreamlike state that nourishes their being at profound levels.

This trance is like the dissociate state—zoning out—except that both partners are together in the altered state of consciousness. They both isolate from the outside world, but they do it together, and they do it deliberately.

PREPARING FOR THE TRANCE

The sexual trance is both a narrowing and a deepening of focus. It is narrow in that it shuts out much of the world. It is deep in that it requires intense focus upon one's lover. The enthrallment is never automatic. The presence of one's lover does not, by itself, create the mood. That requires a shift inside one's own being.

The most important component of this shift is probably anticipation. Unconsummated longing creates sexual tension. The way couples maintain and resolve this tension becomes the raw material of the sexual trance. Sometimes the longing erupts spontaneously; someone wants sex suddenly and for no apparent reason. The desire often fades, of course. However, sometimes it does not. Perhaps days go by and the desire remains just slightly under the surface of everyday life. At other times, someone deliberately cultivates sexual desire because she realizes she will soon have an encounter with her beloved. Whether spontaneous or not, desire becomes longing, and longing seeks resolution. When the resolution does not come, the longing intensifies.

The sexual tension builds, her focus shifts away from other things, and the approaching encounter with her beloved fills her imagination. The trance has begun.

The tasks of daily living require attention regardless of how sexually tense a person may be. Bills must be paid. Children must be fed. Grass must be cut. Life goes on. Although some people can focus on their daily tasks and fulfill their sexual desire at the same time, most of us cannot. For most of us, the sex would not be very satisfying anyway. We would become too much like the woman who asked her husband if he had taken out the trash—while they were having sex!

Preparing for the sexual trance includes taking care of other responsibilities first. If bills are paid, the children are safe, and the grass is cut, nothing serious is likely to happen in the outside world while someone has sex. He becomes free to restrict his world to the one room and the one person who should fill his thoughts during a leisurely, timeless moment of love.

PREPARING THE ENVIRONMENT

A few times in life, a person will experience a powerful sexual moment in less than optimum conditions, such as when teenagers grope around in a car! The movies love these moments. Watching movies, one would think that sex in elevators is a turn-on for most people. Unfortunately, reality is crueler than that! Fantasies not withstanding, elevators and cars are actually poor places in which to make love. Teenagers, who are awash with hormones and fear being discovered, don't need much of an environment to create a sexual moment.

Most of us, most of the time, must prepare our sexual environment. That means that someone must consciously select the materials—the scent, sound, and sight that are conducive to sexual pleasure. A room with a lot of religious paintings or family photographs may not be the best place to make love, for example. A dirty or messy room is not the greatest either. Oh, if we get sexually hungry enough, we can overcome a messy place or less than desirable artifacts. Also, some people may be so aesthetically out of touch that surroundings are not much of a factor. However, the aesthetics of a place will affect most people.

A few candles, a good sound system, a fireplace, a view of a beach or mountains, silky sheets—all these things matter. They affect sexual experience. Someone has to deliberately select and arrange them. Whoever does so gives a gift of awareness and consideration to his or her partner.

A prepared environment helps trigger the sexual trance. In the book of Proverbs, a harlot tempts a man by saying, "I have perfumed my bed with myrrh, aloes, and cinnamon." He can almost smell the incense. He is already under such a spell that the writer must forcibly break with the bad news that the woman enticing him has a husband at home who is good with a bow![3]

The lesson remains: People care about surroundings when having sex. Taking care to prepare them for a time of delight is deeply considerate.

We care about environment because we are not mere spirits. We are material creatures too. The deliberate arrangement of material substances deeply affects our moods and emotions. They help set the stage for enhancing relationships—or they detract from them.

WORSHIP AND THE SHIFT OF CONSCIOUSNESS

Worship is a conscious choice to seek the presence of God and to experience community with other believers. It involves an intellectual, emotional, and physical response to what we encounter through word, sacrament, and fellowship. It requires us to shift our awareness away from everyday matters and toward the eternal perspective. Without awe, we cannot worship because awe is the awareness of God's presence. "He who comes to God must believe that He is."[4]

Worshippers prepare their hearts to encounter God and eternity in many different ways. In a liturgical setting, a worshipper uses prayers that others have written, usually paraphrases of Scripture. She must consciously direct her attention to ponder and process the words she recites. As she adds emotional coloring to the prayers and makes them personally significant, the words create a setting for meeting God and other believers. Without that inner preparation, the service will often feel cold and impersonal; it loses its potential for meaning and purpose.

In a Pentecostal setting, worship does not require the same sort of rational focus as liturgical worship. However, it does require emotional awareness. In a liturgical setting, the touch of water, the taste of wine, or the smell of incense awakens the worshipper's spirit. A Pentecostal environment more forcibly evokes her emotional response. She rarely can be noncommittal about the experience—the setting forces her to respond, either positively or negatively. But in both liturgical and Pentecostal settings, some people "get it" and some do not. For those who do not, the worshippers' movements and words appear meaningless and contrived.

Evangelical worship intentionally addresses the worshipper's rational and conscious self. Therefore, an Evangelical church purposefully uses hymns, sermons, and prayers as vehicles to teach the principles of faith. Seeker-sensitive Evangelical churches work to make connections between believers and unbelievers. However, the spiritual aim remains that of making a rational appeal to the conscious self. In Evangelical worship, the mind is the central gateway to the Spirit.

So churches appeal either to the conscious or to the unconscious; to the rational side or to the emotional or aesthetic side. Few churches seem capable of addressing the need of the whole person. For example, in an Evangelical church, the celebration of Communion often feels awkward because it lacks a context. It can feel as though it has been pasted onto a Bible study or made to serve as a teaching prop. This leaves the celebrants without the means of experiencing the richness of the rite. However, the opposite often happens in a liturgical setting. In that environment, a sermon can feel like an afterthought. The mumbling priest tries to preach but often lacks both knowledge of the Scripture and basic communication skills necessary to deliver it.

In a Pentecostal church, someone can be deeply moved by a sermon but not know exactly why. When asked to explain what the Pentecostal preacher said that seemed so moving at the time, he can be embarrassed to discover that he does not really remember what was said, despite his glowing compliments about the experience.

Each type of worship, then, requires preparation.

Even in private prayer, liturgical, Evangelical, and Pentecostal believers tend to express themselves differently. The believer from a liturgical background will open a prayer book and begin reading slowly and deliberately until her spirit begins to connect to the text. An Evangelical will simply talk to God in a matter-of-fact, conversational tone. A Pentecostal may begin pouring out bits and pieces of disconnected words, interspaced with sighs, moans, and physical movements. All three approaches to prayer are deeply rooted in ancient spiritual practices, but they appeal to different kinds of people. They also require different kinds of preparation.

Couples experience these various forms of communication too. A man and a woman who have intellectual interests may connect very deeply through intense, rational conversation. Dr. Ralph Earle, one of my mentors in therapeutic practice, called this kind of connection "intellectual intimacy." Those who have experienced it know that it can be extremely moving and even emotionally nourishing.

To a couple that enjoys intense sexual experiences with one another, intellectual intimacy may appear empty—a poor substitute for the "real intimacy" that they enjoy. In the same way, different spiritual approaches, even within the same religion, may strike those coming from another perspective as baffling and even meaningless.

The fact is, relationships nurture us in different ways. We need intimate connections for our intellect, our emotions, and our physical being when trying to relate to God or to other people. That's why biblical worship involves word, sacrament, and emotional response. Without any one of these, worship feels perfunctory and empty because it fails to reach the whole person.

When someone deeply involves her whole person in an experience, her perception of the environment narrows. This allows her to focus more intently on her experience. For example, when I read a great book (surely this is happening to you right now!), I become so involved that I may fail to hear someone who is trying to talk to me.

Any experience connected to the wellspring of life requires deep attention. Therefore, one of the most important things we do in life is to learn how to become "ecstatic"—deeply focused on those things that matter the most.

Eight

THINK ABOUT IT!

THE ROLE OF
SEXUAL IMAGINATION

I have always loved the story about two Buddhist monks who had taken vows never to touch a woman. They were walking through the city during a monsoon, and the streets were dangerously flooded. Suddenly, they met a woman who could not cross a wide street because of the water. After hesitating for a moment, one of the monks suddenly picked her up in his arms and carried her across the street.

Afterward, the two monks continued on their way in silence. Finally, the other monk said, "Brother, thou hast touched a woman!"

"Yes," his friend replied, "but I have put her down!"

The point was, one of the monks had touched a woman physically, but he had since detached from her. The other monk had not touched her physically, but he was still deeply connected to her in his imagination.

The story embodies an important truth about sexual life: Sex is mostly a brain activity!

When I was a young minister, I belonged to a Pentecostal group with roots in African-American culture. As the preacher preached, the congregation would shout out, "Amen!" or "That's right!"

Some of the things people said during the sermons became their own unique "signature." For example, a superintendent named Brother Kitchen (he was something like a bishop) would sometimes shout out, "Ahh, think about it!" if a preacher made a moving comment. The preacher would pause for a moment and move on. It was just our superintendent's way of connecting with the preacher and expressing his approval.

One time, though, this remark really broke up the place. We had been listening to a young preacher speak about David's sin with Bathsheba. He was focusing specifically on the moment when the king saw Bathsheba taking her bath on the rooftop.

"Well," he said, "the king was at home while all his soldiers were away fighting the battles of the Lord. There he was, taking it all in, and here was another man's wife, taking a bath up on the roof."

"Oh, my Lord!" someone shouted.

"Yeah, and those soldiers out there were suffering, fighting the battles of the Lord, putting their very lives in danger."

"Uh-huh," another person said.

"Those soldiers were, were…without the, the…the comforts of home," the preacher continued.

"Well!" a lady in the audience said.

The young preacher was becoming visibly upset now. "They, they… well, they, they didn't have the…the…you know…the comforts of home!"

He was stuck on that phrase, "the comforts of home." He just didn't know what to do next, so he was silent for a while.

That's when our dear superintendent let loose with his loud, "Ahh, think about it!"

The trouble was, we were already thinking about it! In fact, we could hardly do anything but think about it!

Sex has a way of capturing one's attention. In a worship setting, that's disturbing. In a relationship, it becomes a vital part of the process.

We prepare for a sexual experience by imagining how it will happen. If we imagine a certain kind of atmosphere, we can plan how to actually create it. If we desire to experience a certain sexual act, we can ask our spouse if he or she agrees. On the other hand, imagining a bad outcome for sex can empower that very experience. So what we imagine about sex matters—a lot!

Without a sexual imagination, a person's sexual life is not going to have much energy. A sexual experience is mental before it becomes physical. Indeed, it remains mental even after becoming physical. And as a memory, it is mental after it is no longer physical. In other words, we anticipate sexual experience in our imagination, we evaluate and explain it in our imagination as it happens, and we recall it in our imagination after it happens.

The more of our senses that we evoke in the imagination, the more vivid our fantasy becomes, and the more intently we can experience our sexual lives. No sexual imagination—no sexual life. Vivid sexual imagination—vivid sexual life. It is as simple as that.

THE SEXUAL TEMPLATE

In large part, we form our sexual tastes in our first experiences with love and arousal.

As an innocent young boy, I was once riding in a car with a preacher's family when he stopped to make a short visit at someone's house. The preacher left me alone in the car with his daughter. When he went into the house, she took my face in her hands and kissed me on the lips. When she did, a freight train ran through me. Angels sang. History stood on tiptoe, and the spirits of dead people danced in the streets. The North and South Poles exchanged places for 60 seconds. When all of that was over, I was no longer a little boy.

I didn't know exactly what had happened; I just knew I wanted more of it! The sexual template was fixed.

We all remember our first sexual awakening. Until that time we are, sexually speaking, like wet clay. The event that births our sexual adulthood becomes like the firing of the clay. Our first sexual experiences thus form many of our desires, attitudes, and sexual preferences. In fact, these preferences may seem to be permanently stamped on our being.

My first sexual experience was heterosexual, and it happened at the expected time of life. Had it been incestuous, homosexual, a rape, or molestation by an older person, my experience would not seem as humorous or innocent. Any of those experiences would have created a much different sexual template for me, and my life would have been much different.

Our sexual template, in turn, deeply influences our perception of our adult self.

Counselors often inquire about a person's sexual history, but not because they think about sex all the time or because they believe that every problem of life is sexual. They ask for sexual history because a person's sexual template reveals so much about how he experiences himself in the world.

For example, I once took the sexual histories of two women in the same day and was amazed how the same event of life had impacted them so differently.

The first lady laughed as she told me about experiencing her first menstrual period.

> I was at school. I had developed later than my friends, who were already having their periods. I had been a bit anxious as to why it hadn't happened to me. Anyway, when it happened, I was delighted. After school, I ran into my house and told my mom. She called my grandmother, who came over to the house and baked me a cake. We sat down and ate cake together while my grandma and mom laughed. Both of them kept calling me a woman.
>
> When I went back to school the next day, I felt different. I knew I wasn't a little girl. It was great!

The next lady's story was strikingly different. She wept as she related the horror of experiencing her first period.

> No one told me what was going to happen. I was scared out of my wits. I mean, here I was, bleeding from my privates.

I was getting ready for school and didn't know what to do. Finally, after dying a thousand deaths, I went in and told my mother that I was "bleeding down there." Mom got a kind of disgusted look on her face—at least it appeared that way to me—and tersely whispered about a blue box in the bathroom.

She told me to look for the box and get "one of the things" from it and to put it inside my underwear so I wouldn't make a mess. Then she told me that this would all happen once a month.

I went to school wishing I could be in Africa or dead. I felt gross. I just wanted the world to go back to the way it had been. I've never really gotten over it.

Those are two radically different responses to the same life event! The reason for the different response is imagination, or the way we explain things to ourselves. The two family's views of life created two different sexual templates. Predictably, the women's views about sex and about life in general evolved quite differently.

Understanding our sexual template is important because that becomes the "default position" that defines the way arousal works for us. Although our sexual tastes and preferences can change, they do so slowly and usually because we have new experiences. However, our first sexual encounters continue to influence us. They become the attitudes and desires that we try to expand, diminish, or overcome for the rest of our lives.

GETTING SEXUAL INFORMATION

For many people, creating a sexual imagination is hardly a problem. Advertisers realize this. They deliberately create images to spark our imagination. That's why they use a picture of a couple in front of a fireplace on a bearskin rug to sell their spark plugs, cars, soap, ice cream, shoes, ink pens, tuna...well, almost anything!

For other people, sexual imagination may be difficult. Thinking about sexual situations, even with a spouse, may seem sinful or dangerous. But we have learned that people who cannot imagine sexual pleasure have difficulty experiencing it. For human beings, the imagination is the center of sexual pleasure

Noted sex therapist Daniel Araoz discovered that people could often overcome their sexual difficulties by simply learning to imagine what pleasurable sex for them would be like. He also found out that the depth and quality of the imagined sexual scene was a predictor of how well the person would do in a sexual experience. For example, if a person could imagine color, texture, taste, scent, or touch in her imagined sexual encounters, she was more likely to report pleasurable sexual experiences later.

Araoz developed a therapeutic method that involved asking a person to imagine a sexual scene of her choice—without asking her to reveal the details. In subsequent sessions, he would ask her to recall the same scene but to add new components that had been missing in earlier visits. For example, he might ask if she could taste what a kiss might be like with her lover or the texture of clothing against her skin.

As a person increased her capacity to imagine sexual experiences, Araoz would ask her to work toward consciously constructing that imagined experience in real life.

THE EFFECT OF PORNOGRAPHY
ON SEXUAL IMAGINATION

From the beginning of time, men and women have used props for intensifying their sexual imagination. Ancient Israelites used the Song of Solomon in this way, so much so that rabbis often forbade unmarried people to read it. The Kama Sutra and other erotic texts of ancient times served the same purposes. However, these erotic texts are not pornographic in the modern sense because they require imagination. More graphic displays of erotica do not.

When our Victorian ancestors uncovered the Roman cities of Pompeii and Herculaneum, they were distressed to discover that almost every home of the noble Romans had sexually explicit pictures and images. The various European governments cooperated to suppress this knowledge about the progenitors of our Western culture.

The advent of photography and motion pictures allowed people not only to make graphic representations of sexual acts but also to actually record them for others to view. This greatly intensified the power and the problem of pornography. It also forced people to define obscenity.

For a Christian, this is a particularly difficult issue. On one hand, tasteful depictions of sexual desire and actions, such as in novels and poetry, can hardly be forbidden on spiritual grounds because we have such a depiction in our own Scriptures. On the other hand, we know that graphic depictions of sexual acts have the potential for twisting and even disordering sexual life. Jesus Himself warns us that to lust is to commit adultery in our heart.[1]

Historically, Christians have tended to depict sexuality in ways that take into account our propensity for addiction to erotic material. For example, John Milton describes the way Adam and Eve make love in the Garden of Eden. He leaves no doubt as to what is taking place, but he artfully maintains a decorum that honors them and us.

A scene in *It's a Wonderful Life* provides a twentieth-century example of this. George Bailey goes into Mary's (his future wife) house while she is talking on the phone with her boyfriend. They have been quarreling in ways that reveal to those of us watching the movie that she is really getting under his skin. As she keeps talking to her boyfriend, George gets continually worked up and moves his face ever closer to hers in order to hear the voice on the phone. As their faces nearly touch and their eyes lock, the tension builds until it becomes nearly unbearable.

It is one of the most erotically charged scenes in cinema. Nonetheless, everyone remains clothed, and the language never degenerates. Perhaps our children and grandchildren can hardly view such a scene as erotic, accustomed as they are to explicit cinematography. Yet, it stands as one of our best examples of erotic depiction that rely on the personal imagination to supply the explicit details.

In the end, every Christian adult is responsible to judge the appropriateness of erotic depictions in literature and art for himself. We are responsible for how such material affects us and how it uses (or abuses) those whom it depicts. Like many other areas of modern life, erotic imagery now offers a level of experience that is barely less than actual flesh-and-blood experiences.

We have to take care with what we allow to touch the wellspring of our life.

That said, every married person has an obligation to his spouse to offer himself in such a way that does not shame, suppress, or punish her God-given desire to connect with her beloved in erotic and romantic passion. Such a connection requires mental as well as genital arousal, so every sexual adult must determine how best to train, manage, and direct his or her erotic imagination.

Think about it!

Nine

TRAINING WHEELS

My friend Samantha is a polite and dignified lady. That's what made her story so funny to my wife and me.

She and her husband, Bert, had traveled to the little town in southern West Virginia where he was raised because his Aunt Gertrude had died. Gertrude's husband, Jack, had died two years before, and they had no children. The old couple had willed their few belongings to Bert.

As Bert and Samantha were sorting through boxes of old letters and bills, Sam suddenly noticed a machine in the corner of the bedroom. It was an old piece of exercise equipment that had been popular many years before, when it had been advertised as a way to lose inches without diet or exercise. It had a place to stand and a wide belt attached to a rather powerful motor. The belt was used as a kind of sling into which the user sat before turning on the switch.

Bert laughed at the apparatus because he remembered his uncle Jack ridiculing his aunt for using it.

"It's as useless as a doorbell on a tombstone," Uncle Jack had said.

"Doctor Randolph told the old woman that it weren't worth nothin', and she ain't lost a pound since we lugged the thing in here. But she goes at it anyway. I leave the house when she does it 'cause it makes such a racket."

Bert said his aunt and uncle had fussed about that stupid machine for years.

As he was telling the story, Samantha decided to try it out for herself. She stood on the platform, sat down in the sling, and turned on the switch. The motion took her by surprise at first. Soon it was shaking her body so strongly that her teeth were vibrating against one another. After just a few minutes of this, Samantha turned red, turned off the machine, and said, "Bert, your aunt was not using this machine to lose weight!"

It took a while for Samantha's words to sink in. He might not have got it anyway except that she had a certain racy look in her eye.

"You've got to be kidding!" Bert said. They laughed so hard they had to take a break from cleaning the house. Then they went out for a cup of coffee.

Well, it's called all sorts of things—sometimes even exercise! The proper name for it is masturbation, and it is a nearly universal human activity. Almost all teenage boys do it. Only 50 percent of teenage girls do it, but by age 50, the percentage has gradually increased until as many women do it as men.

It is one of the few sexual activities that the Bible never mentions, though the book of Leviticus manages to list everything else: no sex with sheep, no sex with mothers-in-law, no sex with a neighbor's wife, no sex with a person of the same gender, and so on. After reading such an inclusive list, one has to conclude that either masturbation wasn't invented yet or it just wasn't that big a deal.

I know that by saying this I am contradicting generations of Christian writers. I don't take that lightly. Nonetheless, I don't see how we can pathologize an activity that seems deliberately created as a safety valve for people who either can't or who choose not to have sex with another person. Making a huge hoopla over masturbation has caused enormous sorrow for far too many healthy, godly, and faithful men and women.

So I chose to call this chapter "Training Wheels" because masturbation is the way most men and women first discover how they function sexually. However, masturbation is also the only legitimate sexual outlet for many widowed, disabled, divorced, and other sexually solitary persons. There are plenty of spiritual issues to consider where masturbation is concerned, as we will see. We just can't honestly consider them until we get real about the subject.

Aunt Gertrude is just not that unique!

In the nineteenth century, American and British culture went to war against masturbation. Dr. John Harvey Kellogg, of cornflakes fame, wanted to see it eliminated from society before his death. In fact, eating cornflakes was supposed to help people resist the desire to masturbate. (When the cornflakes didn't work, he could resort to other means, including surgically removing a young girl's clitoris.) Kellogg's friend, Sylvester Graham, who invented the graham cracker, dedicated himself to the same crusade. As far as we can tell, though, graham crackers were no more effective than cornflakes in stopping people from masturbating. However, we are all doubtlessly thankful for the contribution Kellogg and Graham made to American cuisine!

The Road to Wellville, a 1994 movie starring Anthony Hopkins, is an irreverent satire of Kellogg and Graham's antimasturbation crusade. The movie also shows that these righteous crusaders helped create the climate in which the personal vibrator would be invented. So we might also think of them as the grandfathers of sex toys!

Think about that the next time you eat cornflakes!

A British doctor, Joseph Mortimer Granville, invented the vibrator in 1883 as a medical device for physicians who specialized in "hysteria." In nineteenth-century America, physicians believed that this mysterious disease afflicted hundreds of thousands of women. Many doctors even specialized in treating it. The doctors treated their patients by manually manipulating their genitalia in order to induce a type of convulsion they called "hysterical paroxysm." Afterward, the patient would emerge from the doctor's office to live a normal life until the pressure caused by her disease built up again to unbearable levels.

Granville's new medical device gave doctors a powerful tool for treating these unfortunate women. It also allowed doctors to see many more patients than before. This came as a great relief to the medical community because doctors routinely complained about how much of their time was consumed by treating hysterics.

We can hardly believe that only a few generations ago, doctors could specialize in giving women orgasms. We are even more amazed that the women who went for treatment (and their husbands!) thought they had a disease! To add insult to injury, think of the husbands who paid for those treatments and who were delighted when their wives emerged from the doctor's office so relieved from their hysteria!

Can't you just hear the whispered conversation in the Victorian smoking rooms?

"Well, George, my wife had the same symptoms yours has, but I'm telling you, for days after Georgina sees Dr. Smith, she has the brightest smile on her face! Dr. Smith must be some kind of genius! So take my advice; take Henrietta down to see him. He has a lot of patients already, but I think he'll take your wife in if you'll tell him that I sent you."

Sigmund Freud was one of the doctors who treated hysteria. In fact, he was seeking a cure for the disease when he realized that many of his patients might be suffering from repressed sexual desire! We don't know if his patients found his hypnosis and word association as immediately gratifying as the customary therapeutic treatment with the vibrator, but Freud did manage to create a new field of study!

Obviously, our culture has had a difficult time dealing with masturbation. However, this has been especially true of Evangelical Christians.

In 1979, James Dobson, founder and chairman of the board of *Focus on the Family,* wrote a book on adult sexuality called *Preparing for Adolescence.* He intended to include a chapter on masturbation, but his publisher refused to print it. Amazed at the response, Dobson wrote the following,

> It is my opinion that masturbation is not much of an issue with God. It is a normal part of adolescence…I'm not telling you to masturbate; I hope you don't feel a need for it. But if you do, it is my opinion that you should not struggle with guilt over it. The best I can do is to suggest that you talk to God personally about it.[1]

One can sense Dobson's concern. He doesn't want to needlessly offend his fellow believers, and he certainly doesn't want to contribute to sexual addiction. On the other hand, as a psychologist, he has had to deal with people eaten up with guilt (or even in danger of suicide) because they were having a difficult time dealing with masturbation.

Like most of us who have worked in the mental-health field, Dobson undoubtedly realizes that a religious quest to be asexual beings produces insanity, instability, and deep insecurity. He doesn't want to contribute to that either.

Neither do I! Certainly, masturbation can become an obsession. In fact, it is usually the core behavior in any sexual addiction. As we shall see in another chapter, we must address this issue as well because many people need to discover a way to stop masturbating obsessively. This is not, however, the central problem of most people.

MASTURBATION AND SEXUAL AWAKENING

Men and women become sexually competent by learning how their own bodies and the bodies of the opposite gender function. Usually, people learn about their own body first. However, in those marriages where sex is difficult, one or both of the partners generally lack information and experience about sexual function. Nearly always, the ignorance is about female sexual response, and in many cases, the woman is as much in the dark as her husband.

Boys begin masturbating at puberty, often as the result of a spontaneous and unanticipated nocturnal arousal. He wakes up with an erection and touches himself, more in wonder than for any deliberate purpose. Soon however, nature takes its course, and he experiences orgasm. It is no more complicated than that.

For a male, this is almost a universal experience.

For a female, things are a bit more complicated and less predictable. By middle age, nearly all women have masturbated at one time or another. Fewer women than men masturbate at puberty, however. As a result, many women experience sex with a partner for the first time before having ever experienced solitary arousal and orgasm.

The problem with this is that a woman may be expected to react sexually to her partner before she has even experienced herself as a sexual being. This can be overwhelming and even traumatic. No wonder that some women prefer to avoid sex altogether rather than face the layers of guilt, incompetence, and ignorance that become evident when they are expected to have sex.

For all these reasons, therapists will sometimes talk about masturbation when a couple experiences sexual difficulty.

MASTURBATION IN MARRIAGE

Marylyn had been in therapy for a few months because she rarely had an orgasm. She and her husband had sex several times a month, but it meant very little to her. They had been arguing about that lately because her apathy turned him off. She had taken several weeks to feel secure enough to get to the real issues, however. When she finally told her therapist about her difficulty with having an orgasm, her therapist's reaction surprised her.

"But Marylyn, relatively few women experience orgasm through penis/vaginal contact. Those who do are usually touching themselves."

"What?" Marylyn asked, not believing what she had just heard.

"Women who have orgasms during intercourse usually are stroking their own clitoris at the same time," the therapist said.

"You've got to be kidding," Marylyn said, turning a bit pale. "I don't want to do that," she added as she stared at a small blob of purple in the lower right-hand corner of the abstract painting on the wall.

"Well, that's fine," her therapist said. "You never should do anything during sex that you find uncomfortable. So you don't have to have an orgasm that way. You can decide to have an orgasm some another way. You don't even have to have an orgasm at all if you prefer. However, what I just told you is true."

"I'm afraid I'm just ignorant about sexual things. It's pretty embarrassing," Marylyn added.

"My dear," the therapist assured her, "this is the one area of life that most people think doesn't require training. We are all supposed to know about our own body and our spouse's body by some mysterious infusion of knowledge from the air. You would be shocked at the kinds of things otherwise intelligent people believe about sex.

"For example," he continued, "most people don't even know that you have to tell your partner what you want in bed. Many people get angry when their partner doesn't just give them what they want without asking for it. In your case, you haven't known that it's okay to give yourself what you need in order to have an orgasm during intercourse if that is what you and your husband want to happen."

"What are some other ways people reach orgasm when they're having sex?" Marylyn asked.

"Oh, they do it different ways," said the therapist. "Some women have their orgasm first by having their husbands stroke their clitoris. Others have orgasm during oral sex. But like I said, most women do not experience orgasm during intercourse, even if they enjoy it, unless they touch themselves. So if that is what you are wanting to happen…"

The therapist smiled and looked over at the painting where Marilyn's eyes had been focused.

"I tell you what—if you don't have one already, go buy an inexpensive vibrator. I'll write down some places where you can buy one. Set aside a time when everyone is out of the house and you can experiment. Try touching yourself with the vibrator in a way that feels erotically pleasurable until you have an orgasm. If you do that several times, you will probably have an orgasm each time. It will at least be a way to reassure yourself that nothing is physically wrong with you."

"And if I don't have an orgasm?"

"Believe me, you will unless you become numb because the vibration is set on too strong a setting. If so, just turn it to a less intense setting the next time. Then, when you are comfortable, tell your husband that before you have intercourse, you want him to hold the vibrator in place for a few minutes. When you are quite aroused, go ahead and have intercourse while you hold the vibrator."

"What if he is upset, like...you know...that I don't think he is enough to...you know..."

"Oh, we'll start talking about how to educate your husband about the differences between male and female sexuality," the therapist added. "Most husbands have no problem with that. They're mystified by female sexuality anyway and are delighted when you are sexually fulfilled."

Sex therapists know that a woman is almost certain to have an orgasm if she applies a vibrator on or around her clitoris. That's why many therapists will suggest a solitary moment with a machine when women complain about never having an orgasm. Obviously, having sex with a vibrator is not deeply satisfying at any emotional or spiritual level. However, experiencing an orgasm at all is a powerful therapeutic moment for a woman who has never had one. Once she has an orgasm on her own, by whatever means, she is much more likely to experience one while having sex with her husband.

This means that masturbation is not merely a solitary experience; it can also be a valuable part of one's sexual relationship with another. Although masturbation can be a serious problem when people use it as a way to avoid their need for their partner, most married people continue to masturbate from time to time.

Why? I have no idea. Just knock before you enter the room!

LUST IN THE HEART

Anytime Christians talk about masturbation, we remember that Jesus said that it was not only wrong to commit adultery, it was also wrong to lust for someone. Most people believe that He was speaking about fantasies, in which we imagine having sex with someone in order to stimulate ourselves.

When those words are spoken in church, most men stare straight ahead. Unfortunately, the majority of us are guilty of imagining such things, whether we mean to or not. In fact, it takes a lot of will power not to do it. For most of us, the fantasies are often spontaneous and seem disconnected from our will.

Are such spontaneous scenes in our heads the same thing as lust? If so, then male sexuality, even male biology, seems fundamentally flawed and perverse. In fact, to many men, that often seems to be the attitude of extreme feminists on one hand and Christian fundamentalists on the other. The only solution in that case is to war against all things male because we can only become spiritual (or politically correct) by ceasing to be male.

On the other hand, we must take seriously the fact that our Lord clearly condemns lust. That seems to rule out using fantasies of someone for our autoerotic activities. This means that we must do all we can to exclude real people from our private sexual fantasies. However, having spontaneous and unplanned sexual thoughts about someone is not the same as indulging in fantasies that we deliberately construct and habitually entertain.

So I am claiming that lust is not the same thing as passing interest and arousal, even if it has a specific target. Sexual interest is usually no more spiritually significant than a blast of wind blowing through a tree. Just like the wind, sexual interest is simply nature at work. We all feel its effects, but we also have a choice about what to do about it.

The important thing is to just let the wind blow on by.

THE IMPORTANCE OF ESCAPING THE AUTONOMOUS SELF

The biggest deal about masturbation is that it takes someone further into himself. It requires no stretch toward another person, so it can become a narcissistic act, a refusal to be interdependent with another person. Interpersonal sex involves vulnerability and risk; masturbation involves only one's own imagination and touch. Therefore, it can contribute to a serious withdrawal from real life and a move toward *solipsism,* the belief that we can construct our own reality. Solipsism makes the universe dependent on our imagination. It seduces us into playing God. It is the ultimate masturbation fantasy—self-creation.

Here is the right place to talk about New Age spiritualities that invite us to be the center of the universe. Many spiritual leaders now make a big difference between spirituality and religion. Okay, I get that. To them, religion is about oppressive rules and regulations, and spirituality is a living experience. Were I to sexualize this way of using language, I might say that covenant is about obligation; sex is about life! Put that way, who wouldn't choose sex over covenant?

However, the dichotomy forces one to make a false choice. Religion is about many things, including spirituality. The fact is, spirituality in religion emerges—if it does at all—from a religion's content. I am not a Hindu, but I understand that a Hindu may experience a deep sense of awareness while meditating. However, the Hindu does not meditate in order to feel that awareness; he meditates in order to escape from a false self that separates him from God. A Christian meditates as well, but not to escape a false self (although he may have one); a Christian meditates in order to pull the Word of God deeper into his being. In each case, the spiritual experience is consistent with the path one has chosen to take.

The word "religion" means "binding." This offends modern ears and makes the word an easy target for derision because we do not want to be bound. Therefore, we prefer "spirituality." We want to experience ultimate connection with the Being in a way that quickens and quakes but which does not obligate.

What can we say of a solitary spiritual experience that remains unrelated to the way we think, the way we live, or the friendships we make? It may be gratifying at some level, if it is a good experience, but what difference does it make? At best it is an emotional lubrication, something to help us cope with the frictions of life. That's not unimportant, but if the spiritual world actually exists, one would hope for it to offer us a bit more.

Religion offers theology, or ways to think about the intellectual implications of one's spiritual path. It suggests spiritual habits by which we cultivate the aims of spiritual life in our everyday existence. It invites us into community, where we can continue our spiritual journey in the company of those who share our beliefs and experiences.

Christianity teaches that mere religion is not enough and that it can even get in the way of our spiritual journey. So we somewhat agree with New Age thinkers about the limitations of religion. By replacing relationship with rules, a person can be fooled about where he or she stands with God or with others. Nonetheless, Jesus and the apostles did not mean to suggest that we can make up our own faith as we go, skipping from spiritual experience to spiritual experience. They left us a holy text. They told us to learn about the Scriptures and to pray. They told us to receive baptism and Communion. They urged us to gather with other believers on the first day of the week.

Authentic spirituality, in other words, ought to lead us to community and to covenant. All religions teach such things.

When St. Paul wrote about spiritual experiences, he always pointed people toward community and maturity. For example, he says that if one speaks in tongues, he should do so in private prayer unless someone interprets the message—though it is better to prophesy in one's own language so everyone can understand and judge the word. He goes on to speak of the Lord's body, the members of that body, and how these should work together.

Private spiritual experience can be wonderful and joyful, but what really bears fruit is a commitment to a community of believers.

CONCLUDING WORD

Something is terribly sad about a lonely man sitting at a computer, reading and typing sexual words and becoming increasingly aroused. By what? By bits and bytes of electricity. The pulses of electricity help the lonely man create images in his head with which he becomes enthralled. Deeper and deeper he plunges into self, becoming ever more sexually agitated as he narrows his focus on the mental image he has created for himself and that he will soon discard.

Meanwhile, his wife is waiting for him to come to their bed. She is hoping that tonight he will hold her, that she will not fall asleep alone. *He has so much work to do,* she thinks sadly and then drifts away from another lost opportunity for love.

The years are passing, and with them the chance that this couple will ever truly connect. He is too addicted to his own manufactured reality to actually make love to a flesh-and-blood wife.

God looks at the scene. He wonders at the things people will do in their determination to escape intimacy and relationship. He grieves for a man worshipping idols because the man is afraid to grow up. The man clings to his training wheels, terrified of letting go in order to enjoy the pleasures and responsibilities of adult life. In so doing, he removes himself from the presence of those who love him most in heaven and on earth.

Ten

THE UNKINDLY CUT

Imagine the world in which an ancient Hebrew lived. His own religion taught a restrictive moral code, but the religion of his Canaanite neighbors offered sexual indulgence as worship. As he traveled and traded throughout the region, a Hebrew man passed houses of worship in which priestesses made themselves available for sexual acts.

Now imagine a Hebrew man succumbing to temptation. He enters one of these pagan temples. He nervously approaches one of the temple workers and arranges a sexual tryst. However, when he removes his clothes, the temple worker looks in amazement at his genitals. She has never seen such a sight before, so she calls her coworkers so they can see for themselves the unusual sight of a circumcised man.

He is a Hebrew. He is marked. His sexuality is not his to control. He is a covenant man. As he comes to his senses, he realizes all of this and becomes ashamed. He leaves the pagan temple and returns to his home and to his God.

Circumcision was God's way of claiming the people of Israel at the very source of their biological life. It was His way of saying that covenant children were His before they were even conceived. Sexuality was not an extracurricular activity; it too belonged to God.

Although Christians are not required to circumcise, we do believe all of these things.

This is a core difference between the secular perspective and the Christian one. People talk a lot about their rights over their own bodies. The Christian does not. The Christian believes that the covenant community has a legitimate right to advise us about how to use our bodies. This is a fundamental incompatibility between believers and nonbelievers, and the rite of circumcision symbolized that difference.

WHY GOD SETS BOUNDARIES

The forbidden tree is one of the essential elements in the story of human beginnings told in the first three chapters of Genesis. Even though God had filled the garden with all sorts of plants that were beautiful and nutritious, the forbidden tree quickly captured Adam and Eve's attention.

We are supposed to ask why.

We do not know much about life in Eden before God created Eve. We do know that Adam named all the animals. So we can suppose that as he named them, he became aware of how different he was from them. This distinction made Adam acutely aware of his uniqueness and aloneness. The text implies that Adam began to feel lonely.

God certainly thought it was not good for man to be alone.

God's comment about this provoked Leon Kass, in his book *The Beginning of Wisdom,* to wonder, "Why and for whom is man's aloneness not good?"[1]

In this context, the word "good" was not a moral judgment; it meant simply "complete." Something was good if it was able to fulfill the plan for which God had made it. The rosebush fulfilled its purpose by being beautiful, so God called it good. The river brought nourishment to plants and animals, so God said it was good. But God does not say that man and woman are good, and He specifically says that for man to be by himself is not good.

Adam wasn't bad; he was just not complete. He would not become compete even after the creation of Eve. Man and woman were a work in process, not yet ready to carry out the purposes for which God had made them. Therefore, God was not ready to pronounce them good even after they had each other. In a sense, they were still alone even though they had one another.

Nonetheless, Adam and Eve seemed unaware of their incompleteness. Genesis invites us to contemplate this before we read anything more about human history. We are supposed to understand that this failure to acknowledge imperfection or incompleteness is our core spiritual problem. We are not whole without community. We need God and other human beings. Even if we are single, we have a deep need for community.

Later on, Christ would tell us that this is the essence of God's law—our need for God and for others. However, we often fail to acknowledge this need. We try to insist that we are whole, that we can take care of our needs by ourselves.

In modern language, we call this false sense of completeness "narcissism." That's a word with a great story behind it!

NAUGHTY NARCISSUS

Narcissus was a Greek mythological character who fell in love with his reflection in a pool. When he tried to kiss it and realized it was only a reflection, he killed himself in sorrow.

That's what narcissism means: being so centered upon self that we fail to acknowledge our need of others or to acknowledge how our action and inaction impact others. In the absence of authentic community, we create an image of ourselves that captures our attention and devotion, and that destroys us.

The only thing capable of shattering this false image is community. That is why Adam needed a wife; he needed a relationship that would give him a more accurate reflection of himself than the one he had created in his own heart.

A wife will tell you when your breath stinks. (And if you're not married, your roommate can tell you that!)

Isn't it amazing that you never seem to know that your own breath stinks? And if you can't tell when your breath stinks, how can you know when your behavior stinks? The fact is, you can't tell much about your own behavior if you are constantly looking at your idealized self-image. Unless you have a deep enough relationship with someone who will tell you the truth about yourself, you will remain a prisoner of your narcissism.

So the problem with Adam's aloneness was not just loneliness; it was his sense of self-sufficiency. If left unchecked, it would unravel his humanity.

When no one challenges our self-image, we keep falling, ever deeper, into falsehood, like Narcissus. And then we die.

God created us to be social beings. Our minds and our thoughts develop through social interaction or not at all. Therefore, when we get isolated, we tend to become mentally ill and spiritually damaged. If we are so powerful that no one dares to challenge us, or if we are such a hermit that we don't allow anyone to get near us, we go nuts. We just keep going deeper into our self-delusion. This is our core spiritual problem.

So we need things in our lives that challenge our self-image. This implies that we need restriction and limitation as well as freedom, that we need boundaries as much as we need encouragement and praise. Of course, we don't like limitation and restriction. We want *others* to be restricted in ways that will keep *us* safe, but we do not tend to think that we need restrictions.

That brings us back to the matter of the forbidden tree. Adam and Eve did not seem to notice God's generosity and abundance. They were only paying attention to that one small restriction. Kass notes that "this story focuses rightly upon the one exception to God's generosity, and on the fact of his limitation of human appetite."[2]

Here and elsewhere, the Bible teaches us that unlimited human freedom is as damaging to us as tyranny. Because we are not yet complete, not fully formed, we lack the necessary wisdom to care for ourselves. That's why we often desire things that hurt us or fail to be satisfied with any amount of things we do have as long as there are things that we do not have.

So we need restrictions that will not crush our curiosity or zest for life but that will remind us that we need God and others. We need things in every part of our lives that remind us that God is still forming us from the dust of the earth and that we must cooperate with Him as He does His work in us. That's what holiness is—a focused awareness on the otherness of God and of our need of Him. We need to acknowledge God in order to turn away from our narcissistic trance, from our enthrallment with our own self and its needs.

Kass says that "the turn toward the divine is founded on our discovery of the lack of our own divinity."[3] We are not God, and we cannot create ourselves. We can only surrender to the Creator, who is always willing to shape us and to complete us. If something does not remind us of our lack of divinity, we will not learn to acknowledge the one true God. In other words, we need a symbol of restriction, something that tells us we are not yet complete.

The forbidden tree was probably not a special tree. It was just a tree. However, it was holy—*kiddush*—set apart from ordinary life. In that sense, it was like the Sabbath which appears to be an ordinary day but which is set apart, forbidden for ordinary use. Without the Sabbath, we become workaholics, caught up in a continual spin of doing what we want to do. The Sabbath consecrates a piece of time; it sets a time aside as holy and special, a time not under our control. The prohibition about the tree does the same thing for human appetite. The rite of circumcision does this for our sex drive.

The ultimate restriction upon our appetite is death, of course. Although death is an unpleasant reality and causes us pain, we can view death as a gift. Had God allowed us to live forever as sinful beings, we would have had no barrier to restrain the growth of human evil. Even a powerful Stalin or Hitler must die; they too meet their Maker. Even closer to home, our knowledge of our own approaching death continually calls us to reexamine our purpose and our motivations. No one becomes wise who has not faced his or her own mortality. Without a sense of mortality, we are always ruled by our appetite.

God designed human appetite to seek things that nourish and sustain us. However, because we are not fully formed, we lack the wisdom to know when our appetite stops working for us and begins to work against us.

This is precisely why God gave the covenant sign of circumcision. Having the mark of God on their genitals reminded Hebrew men that their sexual life, which was meant to bring them and their loved one joy and delight, had the potential to destroy them if they didn't learn to contain and manage it.

The New Testament church decided that the rite of circumcision would not be a requirement for Christian discipleship. However, the concept that it symbolized remains vital to spiritual life.

I became aware of this principle early in my married life. I was sitting alone in a restaurant ordering breakfast, and the server was acting very kind to me. My male ego convinced me that she was flirting, and of course, the only thing to do was to reciprocate. So we had this banter going. It wasn't over the line, but it was becoming more intense than it should have.

I clearly recall the moment when I raised my hand to accept the plate of ham and eggs. My wedding band suddenly started gleaming. It seemed to weigh six tons. I panicked. I also had a deep realization that I was getting close to a line that I had drawn by making a covenant just a few weeks before. No harm had been done yet, but it was time to pull back. I was a covenant man.

I had approached the holy thing, the forbidden thing, the boundary that not only restricts life but defines and maintains it.

I pulled back and went home.

SEXUAL BOUNDARIES

The book of Leviticus, the Bible's third book, spends a lot of time on sexual matters. Few people read it though, so I have threatened for years to write a Dr. Seuss–style version of Leviticus. It would go something like this:

> You cannot do it in a boat;
> You cannot do it with a goat.
> You cannot do that here or there;
> You must not do that anywhere.
>
> Do not do it with a sister
> And not with the babysitter.
> Do not do it with a brother
> And not with your husband's mother.
>
> Stop that! Don't! You should know better!
> Don't do it with an alligator.

Okay, the alligator is over the top. Even the book of Leviticus doesn't consider that a possibility, but you get the idea. Leviticus does seem to go on and on, prohibiting endless kinds of sexual unions. Earlier generations of commentators sometimes wondered why these prohibitions were necessary.

Well, they were necessary because people are inclined to do them (though hopefully not with an alligator). God forbids them, not because He wants to spoil our fun but because illicit unions destroy the fabric of family, society, and culture. They also destroy the structure of the individual psyche.

An incestuous union, for example, destroys a family relationship. If the relationship between a brother and sister becomes sexual, it ceases to be a brother-sister relationship at all. If some relationships are not sexually off-limits, we are never free to step out of our sexual role in order to relate to others in some other fashion. Sexual union, however intimate, colors a relationship in way that cannot be undone.

C.S. Lewis predicted that the culture's growing acceptance of homosexuality would probably make it difficult to form significant same-gender relationships. He wrote this in the same spirit that the movie *When Harry Met Sally* explored whether men and women could be friends. If a friendship may turn sexual at any moment, it cannot avoid the powerful influence of physical attraction, sexual posturing, and so forth.

All of this is true for any relationship, as codes of ethics in our various professions recognize. A doctor-patient relationship mutates if it becomes sexual. A professor-student relationship deteriorates if it becomes sexual. Sex highjacks the original purpose of a relationship and permanently alters it. That is why we protect those relationships by law and by drafting codes for professional ethics.

Leviticus is right, not just because it is a religious document but because it accurately describes the boundaries that sustain, nurture, and define sexual life. Circumcision, like the ring on my finger, reminds me to keep away from the line.

HOW RESTRAINT CAN INTENSIFY EXPERIENCE

I had just taken my seat in the human sexuality class that was required for my psychology degree. I was also nervous. Rumors had it that this class was quite explicit and that the teacher was determined to loosen everyone up. As an Evangelical pastor, I was not sure I wanted to be loosened up! As I looked around at the 15 other people in the class and then back at the teacher, I wondered what was going to happen.

"Welcome to the famous sex class!" our teacher began. "You are all training to be psychologists and therapists. Whether you realize it or not, your work will directly or indirectly involve sexual issues more than any other single thing. That's why you are here.

"Some of you will find things you learn in this class upsetting. Some of it will be titillating. Some of it will be amusing. Some of it will be boring. However, you will also have all of these responses as you encounter your various patients. If you can't handle this class, you probably can't handle this career.

"The first thing we are going to do," she said, "is learn how to eat an M&M."

At that, she began to pass out a bag of candy. She then asked each of us to take one piece of candy from the bag and to hold it in our hands until receiving further instruction.

Now I was really nervous. This was a sex class. What, pray tell, were we going to do with the M&M?

When we all had a piece of candy, she began to speak softly.

"Please put the M&M in your mouth. Don't chew it or swallow it, though. Just hold it in your mouth as I continue to talk to you.

"You have all driven here tonight through the traffic. You are tired. Your minds are not quite here yet. You are also nervous about this class. You are not sure you will be comfortable with what you think I will be teaching you. But tonight you will learn a lesson you will never forget—about sex, about life, and about the mind.

"We do not know how to eat. We grab a fistful of M&M's and cram them in our mouths. Later, our stomachs hurt, and we become angry with ourselves for having eaten so much. Sadly though, while we are actually eating the candy, we didn't even taste the M&M's.

"Are you noticing now that the chocolate has begun to coat your mouth? Can you taste, really taste that little burst of flavor? Now, don't swallow the chocolate just yet. Allow it to keep coating your mouth and tongue. Isn't it something, how flavorful one M&M can be?

"Many people try to increase their sexual pleasure by doing bizarre things to themselves and to others. They want three partners or an orgy. They want to do it in a plane or in a closet at work. But you know what most people really want? They want to experience intimacy with another person. And that doesn't happen through intensity or novelty. To experience intimacy, we have to learn how to taste and to savor simple experience. That requires us to slow down and to focus, just as we have been doing with this M&M. All the rest is just anatomy."

I left the class that night transfixed by her lesson. I not only lost 30 pounds in the following months but also learned that increasing pleasure does not depend on creating more sensation. Increasing pleasure requires us to focus fully upon the pleasure already available to us.

Pleasure, sexual or otherwise, is not about quantity of experience but about the respect, attention, and interpretation we give to the experience we already have. This is why sex therapists will often ask a couple who is having sexual difficulty to stop having sex for a specified amount of time.

Fred and Regina's therapist did that. They had been at odds with one another about their sex life.

"He wants it every day," she complained, "whether I'm sick, well, tired, or simply not interested. I feel used, ignored, and frustrated with him. If I could detach my breasts and let him play with them while I go watch TV, I would. I doubt he would even notice I was gone!"

"Wow, that's cruel," Fred said spiritedly. "I have never wanted to use you that way. We used to enjoy sex. The problem is that now you never seem to want it. I'm feeling frustrated and rejected, and I'm starting to get bitter about it."

After hearing about their different perspectives for a couple of sessions, Donald, their therapist, approached them with an idea: "I think you should both agree not to have sex for six weeks while we keep meeting once a week."

"Well, we know whose side you're on!" Fred blurted out. "I guess you think I'm just an oversexed moocher of some sort."

"So you feel hurt by my suggestion?" asked Donald.

"Of course I do. You've missed the whole point. I'm not trying to just have sex. I want us to have what we once had—loving fun and desire for one another."

"How about you, Regina?" Are you willing to try this?"

"I'm willing to try it, but I'm concerned that you've hurt Fred. I didn't mean to make him out to be a bad person. I'm here because I love him, and he is always tender and kind to me when we have sex. I don't want to drive him away. I know plenty of women at his work would be glad to have sex with him!"

"Gosh, Regina," Fred interjected, "I don't want to have sex with anyone else. I'm telling you, neither you nor Donald are understanding me!"

"It's always possible that I don't understand you, but I think I do. Why not try it? As we proceed, I really believe that both of you will come to understand some things that you may not learn any other way," Donald said.

Regina and Fred reluctantly agreed to abstain from sex for the six weeks of therapy.

Four weeks later, as the session began, Regina asked to speak first.

"Something happened this weekend that I need to own up to," she said. "We were lying in bed, talking about our life and about how difficult it had been to come to therapy. Neither of us quite understood what you are trying to do with this whole abstinence thing. Fred told me that it was difficult for him not to have sex. However, he said he was willing to even go longer with the period of abstinence if it would help us and if that's what I wanted.

"'Actually, I've wanted sex this week,' I told him.

"'Really?' he said, sitting up in the bed.

"'Really!' I responded.

"When I saw tears in his eyes, I realized that something more than sex had been going on. So I kissed him. Soon things got kind of…you know…So he said, 'We have to stop. We promised Donald…'

"'He's not here!' I said. Then I kind of pushed the envelope, and we had sex. Twice. It's my fault. He would have kept the promise if I had not pushed it."

"Sounds like you wanted to have sex and that you enjoyed it. Is that right?" Donald asked.

"Well, yes, I did, but I was worried that it might harm whatever you're trying to do with the whole abstinence thing," Regina replied.

"And how about you, Fred? How did you feel about what happened, and what do you feel today?" Donald asked.

"Obviously, I liked it," Fred said with a big grin. "Right now though, I feel sort of like a little boy who did something he shouldn't have done."

"What was different about having sex last Saturday night than how you have experienced it for the last year or so?" Donald wanted to know.

"Well, for me, I didn't feel obligated," Regina replied. "I knew that if I had stopped with the kissing, Fred would have been frustrated but not mad at me. Actually, he would have blamed you, Donald," Regina laughed. "Also, I felt warm and connected to Fred because he was wrestling with his own feelings in order to figure out what he needed to do to make me feel safe and loved."

"And you, Fred?" Donald asked. "How was it different for you?"

"I felt invited," Fred said. "When I offered to pull back and she kept encouraging me to keep going, I realized that it was something she wanted."

"Very well," Donald said. "We'll spend the next couple of weeks talking about how respecting boundaries and honoring the rhythms of life make sexual life healthy and intense. We are making progress."

Fred and Regina were experiencing the power of boundaries to create rhythm and passion. This is the spirit in which the Bible sets sexual boundaries and prohibitions. It sets boundaries not only to keep us from having sex with the wrong people but also to help our sexual lives remain meaningful and intense.

Consider the Levitical prohibitions against sex during menstruation, for example. Many feminists are offended at this prohibition, as if it were an insult to women: Men can't have sex with a menstruating woman because she is nasty. There is, however, another way to look at it.

Author Wendy Shalit recounts why she had decided to observe her Jewish religion's prohibition against having sex during her period. Although she is a young woman who defines herself as a feminist, she rejected the idea that this prohibition insults women. She discovered that taking a week's break from her otherwise active sexual life allowed her and her husband to renew the intensity of their sexual lives. The time-out—a kind of a Sabbath—brought rhythm into their lives that had been missing. The restriction seemed to heighten their sexual energy rather than to dampen it.[4]

Her observation affirms the biblical principle of imposing rhythm on life. There is a time to dance and a time to refrain from dancing, a time to sow and a time to reap, a time to embrace and a time to refrain from embracing. Every few years, the fields must be left alone to renew themselves. Every few years, debts must be forgiven so the community can begin anew. In certain seasons, one should not eat things with yeast. All these teachings about prohibition and restriction, which in youth we are prone to ridicule, turn out to be the very things that rekindle life.

For the Christian, nature can be out of control because it is damaged and disordered. Circumcision is a symbol that reminds us that restraining nature's appetite is a way that we manage and direct nature. In so doing, we reap the benefit of healthy nature.

Eleven

CAN'T GET ENOUGH

THE BONDAGE OF SEXUAL ADDICTION

I met Bill Canterbury in graduate school, where he and his wife, Rebecca, were training to become therapists. They told me their story one evening over a cup of coffee. They had been Sunday school teachers in a Baptist church just a few blocks from where we were meeting. In fact, they had met in a teachers' seminar at the church a couple of years before.

One evening after the seminar, Bill and Rebecca had decided to go out to a Mexican restaurant. After a salad and some flan, they went to her apartment. One thing led to another, and they had sex later that night.

They quickly discovered that they were both sexually adventurous, and as the weeks went by, they kept pushing the boundaries. First, they watched a lot of porn. Then, they began acting out some of the things they had watched. One evening, they found themselves cruising the highway, doing various sexual acts in their car while other drivers—particularly truck drivers—watched. They did this for a number of weeks.

Their risky behavior ended one evening after they pulled into Rebecca's driveway. As they were getting out of their car, a police car pulled behind them. A police officer got out of the car and informed them that they were under arrest for reckless endangerment and public indecency.

As it turned out, there would not be enough evidence to actually convict them. However, they endured several weeks of questioning, during which time they realized that they needed help.

They had gotten married while on a weekend trip to Las Vegas before the night the police car showed up. Despite their disordered beginning, they desperately wanted to find a way to build a wholesome life together, and marriage seemed the best place to start.

After a few months of marriage, they decided to make an appointment with a pastor at their church. He listened to their story with compassion, and amazingly, he kept it confidential. He introduced them to the writings of Patrick Carnes, the noted expert on sexual addiction. He also encouraged them to join a 12-step group that focused on sexual issues. He didn't pull any punches; he told them that they were out of control and were in serious danger. Unless they got serious about recovery, they would probably act out again.

The pastor called them once a week to make sure they were going to meetings. He also kept introducing them to people he believed could help them. They both went through a couple of years of counseling with separate therapists, joined separate therapy groups, and finally worked with a couples' therapist. In time, they also decided to get professional training so they could better understand what they had experienced and, perhaps, so they could prepare themselves to help others.

Now, many years later, Bill and Rebecca work with teenagers who struggle with drug addiction. The members of the church they now attend have no idea that this well-dressed, conservative couple used to expose themselves on the interstate that runs in front of their church property.

"We were idiots," Rebecca said. "For some reason, while we were acting out like that, we felt higher than kites. It's really embarrassing now; I know we could have been killed or killed someone else. But I realize that we could act out again if we don't stay focused and accountable. Addiction is not something that you reason out. It takes over if you give it an opportunity."

"We are committed to HALT," Bill added.

"HALT?" I asked, "What does that mean?"

"It means Hungry, Angry, Lonely, and Tired," Bill replied. "If we experience any one of those things, we can get in trouble. Two or more of them and we're dead meat! We're recovering sex offenders, but God saved our lives. He gave us a chance for a normal life. We don't want to blow it."

THE ADDICTIVE CYCLE

Earlier in this book, we talked about the importance of sexual imagination. In that chapter, I was mostly emphasizing the positive side of imagination. We saw that sex is mostly a brain activity and that without focused imagination, sex becomes a simple physical activity that most people find dissatisfying. Imagination is a double-edged sword, however. Sexual imagination—fantasy—is also the fuel of sexual addiction.

Human beings were not created to be angels. We are material beings. Therefore, every belief, fantasy, and desire seeks embodiment, to be "made flesh." People who are consistently exposed to sexual stimulation can become prisoners of their own imagination. They can become driven to act out the fantasies they habitually imagine. Furthermore, if people become sexually addicted, their fantasies tend to grow increasingly bizarre and twisted.

When people's actions become disconnected from their value system, they must dissociate from reality in order to do them. They will think, *I'm not really doing these things. The devil (or my sinful flesh) is overpowering me.* That doesn't stop them from doing the things they disapprove of; it just makes them unconscious as they do them! They stop taking responsibility for their actions. They live a double life.

Like most addicts, Bill and Rebecca sometimes felt terribly ashamed of their actions and promised themselves that they would not do those crazy things again. Their promises led to seasons of repression and to a temporary return to their religious convictions. While in that religious phase, they would deny their steadily building sexual tension. However, the tension would inevitably explode into another fury of dissociated sexual activity. They couldn't control the addiction by themselves.

No one can!

Bill and Rebecca were running through the addictive cycle:

1. acting out

2. shame and regret

3. promises and repression

4. angelic behavior accompanied by denial of desire

Sooner or later addicts will confront a trigger—some event, mood, or situation that provokes them to enter the trance. They will act out again in denial and defiance of their reason.

Bill and Rebecca continued this dance until they made an ironclad commitment to fully disclose their addiction and to turn their lives over to the care of God.

They are a courageous couple. Their humility and continued commitment to seek spiritual and emotional health has molded them into people of great wisdom and enormous grace.

Bill and Rebecca's story of addiction is, unfortunately, common. The details vary, but similar scenarios abound in this age of autonomy and social disconnection. Ours is, after all, the age of addiction.

Sexuality, being the earthy, bodily experience that it is, promises like few other experiences to release us from the prison of ourselves. It offers us a way to connect deeply with another person. However, when people's sexuality has been damaged for some reason, finding relief in secret and solitary experience (such as Internet sex) can be easier than facing all the scary stuff that sex with another person entails. Sex thus becomes a way to anesthetize their pain instead of a connection with another person.

Sometimes, as in Bill and Rebecca's case, addicts feel as if they are with another person. Not really. The partner is actually a prop, a way to access their drug of choice. Bill and Rebecca were really alone, as all addicts are.

SEXUAL IMAGINATION AND ADDICTION

We are spiritual as well as material beings. This reality is the cause of much of the tension in our lives. Because we are spiritual beings, we can conceive ideas and scenarios that are too powerful, too beautiful, and too perfect to exist in a material world. Becoming a healthy spiritual person includes learning to accept and even to appreciate the limits of our material world. We learn to accept what one writer called a "spirituality of imperfection."[1] We learn to take pleasure in being a spiritual and material person at the same time. We learn to accept the reality of our physical and limited universe.

Although we share with God the power to envision "those things which do not exist as though they did," we do not share His power to speak such things into being.[2] We may use our imagination to conceive things that we can depict in the material world through our work, such as when we write fantasy literature or draw pictures of unicorns. However, only God could actually create a unicorn in the material world.

This limitation of our creative powers can frustrate us because we are capable of imagining things that we cannot actually bring into being. The human imagination (the word means "image making") can create a rose. It can imagine the sensation of touching its imaginary petals, smelling the scent of its imaginary perfume, and even feeling the prick of its imaginary thorn. However, an imaginary rose will not satisfy us for long. We are unavoidably material creatures. We want more than mental abstractions. We want to touch and to smell a real rose. To do that requires us to surrender our insistence upon perfection. A real rose is less perfect than our imaginary rose.

Perfectionism is the insistence that what I see in my head must become what I experience in the material world. The problem with this is that the things in my head are exactly the way I want them to be. Things in the world, however, are only *somewhat* the way I want them to be. Therefore, if I cling to the notion that my mental abstractions must become reality, I doom myself to a continual disappointment with the world as it actually is.

The rose in one's head has no thorns. The ones in nature inevitably do!

The partner in someone's head has no faults. Understandably then, his imaginary partner is easier to deal with than the real thing. That's why we tend to create an imaginary partner. An imaginary partner, after all, has no real needs of her own. In contrast, one person's real-life partner cannot fully understand what we need. Even worse, a flesh-and-blood partner may choose not to meet those needs even if she does understand them. All this makes our imaginary partner safer than the flesh-and-blood kind.

Ned Baker talked about this one night with his accountability group.

"I have no idea why I spent all of my money on that Internet site," he said. "A part of me knew that the woman I was writing to couldn't be everything she claimed. I mean, for all I know she could have been lying about the fact that she was even a woman, like that mechanic up in New Jersey. He had all those rich CEOs fooled into paying him big bucks for sex talk on the phone!

"Why do we let ourselves get fooled like this?" Ned asked. "We're surrounded by women who want a relationship—my own wife kept begging me to get real with her—but we fall for these kinds of scams. It's so humiliating!"

Ned asked a good question. One may imagine a sexual experience in the privacy of his or her own head that unites body, soul, and mind in a great burst of cosmic consciousness. Sex with a flesh-and-blood partner may feel a little bit like that a few times in life. However, perfectionism cannot settle for "almost" or "pretty good." It's all or nothing. Therefore, the perfectionist expects to experience in the material world that which he imagines. This is a recipe for disappointment and disillusionment, and it leads to addictions.

And the problem with perfectionism doesn't end there. Think about what happens if we demand that a person *not* imagine a rose, *not* feel its petals, *not* smell its perfume. The demand empowers the concept it forbids. That is what happens when a religious perfectionist forbids herself to think about sex. Her attempts to repudiate sexuality actually empower her sexual obsession.

As we have been seeing, we are inescapably sexual beings. Regardless of how devout we become, most of us must deal with sexual desire from time to time. If we deny this, we get into trouble. In fact, the hunger for intimacy that fuels our longing for God is exactly the same force that motivates us to know another human being. That is why spiritual people have a notorious propensity for acting out sexually. When the connection between sex and spirit is honestly and openly accepted, both sexuality and spirituality can thrive in a healthy way. However, when this fact of human life is suppressed and denied, it can cause all sorts of evil, especially in those who most vigorously seek to please their own inner judge (whom they may call "God").

Perfectionism, then, whether it attempts to destroy sexuality or to enshrine it as an idol, poisons life. Sex is not a great web of wickedness, nor is it a conduit to cosmic consciousness. Sex is not Satan, nor is it God. Sex is just sex. It is, to be sure, one of the great pleasures of life, but healthy sexuality cannot survive when we try to push it to either perfectionistic extreme.

THE COADDICT

Most addicts manage to find people to take care of their everyday lives for them while they play. These people enable the addict to avoid facing his issues, keeping him from hitting the bottom and delivering him from the consequences of his actions. Rebecca and Bill discovered that she was really a coaddict, more driven to empower his addiction than to act out for her own benefit.

What motivates a coaddict? Usually, the coaddict herself calls it love.

The coaddict is the member of the addict's network of family and friends who works to cover up the addict's actions. Sometimes, the coaddict even takes the blame for the addict's actions or actively participates in them so she doesn't lose the addict's love.

Mary Jones remembers that when her father would beat her mother, her mother would usually talk to her and her sisters the following day, saying something like this:

"Your dad has been working really hard, and I pushed him over the edge last night. I should have fixed the dinner the way he wanted it instead of making a scene like I did. I know he doesn't like potatoes the way I fixed them. That's what made him so mad. After working so hard all day, he came home ready for a good meal, and I ruined it for him.

"Your dad is a good man. He works really hard. So don't say anything about what happened last night to any of your friends. People won't understand what your dad goes through. If people start gossiping about your dad and it gets under his skin, he might just pack up and leave. Then what would we do?"

The coaddict thus supports and empowers the addict.

A sex addict usually constructs a supportive system around himself, similar to the one that Mary Jones describes. Often, a coaddict is a spouse.

"I realized that my husband was doing something," a woman once told me. "When he traveled, he had expenses that didn't make sense to me. But I always believed his stories. When my gynecologist told me I had a sexually transmitted infection, I decided to believe my husband's story that he had read on the Internet that sometimes the infection can spread through exercise equipment! Something in me just didn't want to believe that he was seeing prostitutes. If he hadn't gotten fired for using company money for that seminar in Dallas when he actually hadn't attended a single session, I would never have woken up. I almost believed his lies even about that!"

"Have you ever heard of Marilyn Murray's circles of intimacy?" I asked.

"No. Who is she?" the woman replied.

"She has helped a lot of people through the years discover why they have enabled addicts in their lives, all in the name of love," I said. "She used to draw circles, one inside the other, to represent the human personality. She would say that the center circle represents the most intimate place of your life. That is the circle you should share with God—only Him. The next circle is for your spouse (or for a single person's parents). After that is a circle for family members. Then, one for friends. Next is for acquaintances. She called her drawings the circles of intimacy.

"Marilyn used to say that when a person gets addicted, he allows his addiction to occupy the innermost circle. So the addiction becomes a god. Even the addict is not in his circle after a while. That's why he will destroy his health or livelihood in pursuit of his addiction. When you're trying to relate to a person like that, he's not even home. You are really relating to a chemical—or in your case, to sexual experiences with prostitutes, the Internet, and what have you. It's a real sick deal."

"But why?" she asked. "I gave Henry all the sex he wanted."

"It's not about that," I said. "He didn't want sex as a way to connect to you. He wanted sex as a drug. It was the danger, the private nature of the experience, the adrenaline he sought.

"The truth of the matter is this: He wanted sex without intimacy because the intimacy was the very thing he feared."

THE ADDICTIVE SYSTEM

One of Aristotle's most perceptive statements was that human beings are social animals. In other words, personhood is formed by a community and must be sustained by it. Even those hermits of history whom we admire—the desert fathers, Henry David Thoreau, and so forth—were formed by the cultures from which they separated. These seemingly isolated souls were emotionally and intellectually sustained by the writings of those communities. Furthermore, we admire these people because they connected with us through their books of enduring worth.

Millions have read *Walden,* Thoreau's great masterpiece on the blessings of solitary life. He was able to write it because someone taught him to write. Thoreau then read what others had written, reflected on the thoughts he encountered in those writings, and wrote down thoughts of his own for us to read. We call that a conversation.

Thoreau was hardly self-produced. He was an interesting individual, to be sure. However, he, like all of us, was a product of his culture and society. That is an example of what Aristotle meant when he asserted that humans are social animals.

As Daniel Siegel so ably describes in his books, discoveries made in the field of neuroscience in the past decade clearly reveal how communities influence even our physical brains and nervous systems. They certainly mold the way our mental processes work.

We learn to think by conversing with the members of our family of origin. After all, what is conscious thought if not an internal conversation with ourselves? By conversing with others, we learn how to allow different opinions to debate one another in the privacy of our own heads. (I never lose an argument when I have imaginary debates with my wife!)

We also learn from others how to label and express our emotions. In one family, crying means "I am hurting and need to share that with someone." In another family, it means "I am too weak to handle real life." Not surprisingly, a person raised in the first family cries when dealing with stress and grief. One raised by the second family will probably not even consider crying. He may throw things instead.

Yes, we are social animals. We are fragments of our families of origin. We live and act in the world, interpret life, and express ourselves in ways that are consistent with the script that our father, mother, sisters, and brothers gave us when we were children. This has serious implications for addicts.

An addiction becomes a living presence of its own, taking up residence at the core of a family. It rules the addict and, through him, all those who are connected to him. Family members and friends are thus spiritually connected one to the other. Every family has a "wireless router" through which viruses move and then take root in everyone connected to that system. Furthermore, the connection reaches not only through space but also through time. The same addiction can thus infest a family for generations. It is a parasite. It mutates, reproduces, and infects new victims as the host family cultivates fresh blood to sustain it.

STARTING OVER

Will McConnell now understands how addiction works. Before his conviction for malpractice, he was a successful dentist. He had a practice in a medium-sized town in the American West, where he grew up. He was handsome, courteous, and easygoing. People usually liked him. He had no difficulty keeping clients.

Will's wife had suspected for years that he had been sexually active with some of his dental assistants and clients. However, most people who knew him, including his children, believed her accusations to be unfounded. Even when a woman first filed a sexual harassment suit, Will's friends believed him when he denied it. Within weeks however, another woman joined the first. Soon there were five. Then rumors and innuendos spread from dozens of women, all claiming that they either had been propositioned or had actively participated in some sexual action while in Will's office for dental work.

The suits were financially disastrous for the McConnell family. They eventually declared bankruptcy. Because some of the cases involved illegal use of drugs, Will had to serve time in a minimum-security facility. After his release, he also gave nearly three years of community service to a nearby reservation.

Will's wife filed for divorce while he was incarcerated. But before the divorce became final, she agreed to stop the proceedings if he could demonstrate to her that he was seriously working toward recovery. She did not promise that she would ever allow him to move back in with her, however. They merely continued to talk and occasionally to meet for dinner.

Will did get serious about counseling. He met a group of therapists who had been influenced by Patrick Carnes. They had a compassionate but no-nonsense approach to sex addiction. In the course of his treatment at their facility, Will began to talk to his sisters. He also began talking to an uncle whom he had not seen for many years. He discovered some things.

Before he was born, Will's father had become an itinerate preacher in North Carolina. Will had not known his father because his mother had left and moved west when Will was only six years old. He saw his father only a few times after that. Once, after Will had become a dentist, his father had called, asking for help with his ministry. When Will's mother passed away, his father called to offer condolences and told Will how proud he was of him before hanging up. A few years after that, he found out that his father had died as well.

Will's uncle told him that his father had been kicked out of his denomination shortly after Will was born because of sexual improprieties of some sort. Afterward, he began preaching on the radio. He was able to make a living from people's donations to that broadcast. Later, he expanded his program to several stations in western North Carolina. He also traveled throughout the region, preaching at small churches, saving souls, and collecting funds as he went. Rumor had it that the old preacher had left behind as many children as converts.

Will's mother never married again. She did, however, have many friends, male and female, who shared her hospitality for extended periods. Will does not recall witnessing anything that he deems improper from his mother, however. She kept him clothed, fed, and in school. She also insisted that he get a good education and make a life for himself.

Will's older brother entered the military at 18 and decided to make a career in the United States Marines. His younger sister, who married at 19 and had four children, converted to Mormonism. His relationships with both siblings remained cordial but distant.

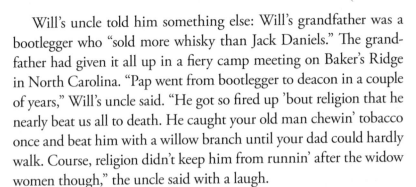

Will's uncle told him something else: Will's grandfather was a bootlegger who "sold more whisky than Jack Daniels." The grandfather had given it all up in a fiery camp meeting on Baker's Ridge in North Carolina. "Pap went from bootlegger to deacon in a couple of years," Will's uncle said. "He got so fired up 'bout religion that he nearly beat us all to death. He caught your old man chewin' tobacco once and beat him with a willow branch until your dad could hardly walk. Course, religion didn't keep him from runnin' after the widow women though," the uncle said with a laugh.

Little by little, Will discovered that many of his uncles, aunts, grandparents, and cousins, had struggled with addictions. Some were religious fanatics, some were alcoholics, some gambled, and others cheated on their spouses. Those who seemingly escaped their family madness, did so by following rigid systems within narrowly defined communities. There was not much health in the McConnell clan.

In the course of his treatment, Will began attending a small Bible study group called the Alpha Course near his home. As the weeks passed, he felt free to share his story. He was surprised that it seemed to make no difference in the way the other members of the group responded to him. One night, he announced that he was thinking about becoming a Christian, though he feared his family tendency of swinging from sinner to saint and back to sinner again.

The other members of the group told Will to take his time, to think it over. He was their friend whether he ever converted or not.

A few weeks later, someone talked about the story of Abraham. They said that Abraham had heard a call from God to leave his father's house. The words seem to pierce Will's soul. He decided the time had come for him to leave his own father's house. A full 50 years had passed since his mother had carried him across the continent, trying to leave his dad. Will wondered, *Can someone leave the place where his family lives without leaving its values and dysfunction? If I become a Christian, will I just be perpetuating the same mindless cycle that con artists in my family have been performing for generations?*

He talked to his therapist about that. When he left the session, he felt that what he really wanted to do was to find a new community of solid people who seemed to be living the way he wanted to live. Also, he needed a sense of supernatural grace to empower his decision to live a new kind of life. He had been reading the book *Mere Christianity* and had concluded that new life was possible for him. However, he felt that he needed to act in some public way without grandstanding.

A month later, Will was baptized. His wife read a Scripture passage just before he went into the water. As he walked out of the pool and on the grass, he could feel his bare feet touching the soil. He looked at his wife. Then he looked beyond her to his 19-year-old daughter. Both of them were smiling at him.

The next afternoon, he went to his addiction support group. He checked in with the other members of the group.

"It's been a good week," he said. "I have made a choice that I believe will change my life. I am a bit apprehensive because I have the ability to deceive myself. However, I have asked for the help of God and for the help of my friends. So I will take it a day at a time. Also, I want to report, I have something to look forward to this week. Thursday, I am having lunch with my daughter. Life is good."

"Thanks, Will," said the compulsive gambler.

He looked around and saw several nodding their heads.

"Thanks for sharing," the facilitator said. "Keep coming to the meetings."

Twelve

CAN'T TOUCH THIS

The first time I met him, James Harrison was deeply hurt and bewildered. Darlene, his wife of 20 years, was about to divorce him, and he couldn't understand why. He was an effective and much-loved clergyman, and his charisma and grasp of Scripture made him a compelling speaker. Furthermore, unlike many preachers, his personality was much more than a mere stage presence. His parishioners nearly all described him as a kind and considerate person, "a real gentleman" as one older lady put it.

Nonetheless, Darlene wanted out.

When I first heard his story, I couldn't keep from feeling angry with Darlene. James was obviously a good man. What in the world was wrong with her?

However, as is often the case, I had not heard the whole story.

When I saw Darlene, she began by agreeing with her husband's assessment of their situation.

"I'm the problem," she said. "James is the sort of man women die for. I watch those church women looking him over, and I know what they're thinking. They would like to take him home with them. And why not? He's courteous, he always treats women with respect—I mean, gosh, he opens doors for me and all that stuff. He's wonderful. I completely understand why women look at him the way they do."

Now I was really confused. What *did* this woman want?

"Dan, I'm really embarrassed to tell you what my issue is with James. It seems so trivial and unspiritual. But…well, I've tried, but I just can't stop wanting to have some sort of sexual life."

"So you don't have sex?" I asked.

"Well, no, I can't say that we don't have *any* sex…it's more complicated than that. We go for a long time without sex, usually one or two months. Then one evening, the mood will hit him. He'll start sending out the signals that he wants to make love, but he's like a guilty little boy. He's almost apologizing as he comes on to me. When I respond, he acts like a thirsty man in the desert running toward an oasis. He goes crazy for a few minutes, and then it's all over.

"Here's the weird part: When he's finished, he doesn't say another word. He goes into his home office and studies his Bible and prays for hours. Sometimes I can hear him praying fervently. But I feel angry, used, and abandoned. One night—gosh, I can't believe I'm telling you this—I started to masturbate, and I just got so angry about having to do that while my husband was in the next room. I was so humiliated at him, at myself. Then I heard him praying. I felt like a slut. In fact, I just kept hearing the word 'whore' repeated over and over in my head.

"I'm probably oversexed or something, but I can't help it. I just can't keep this up. I'm mad at the church and probably mad at God. I don't want to hear hymns or prayers. To tell you the truth, a part of me sometimes would like to have an affair with someone who would just enjoy making love to me without guilt.

"So there it is. Evidently, I'm just undisciplined and unspiritual."

After I had met with James and Darlene several times, I came to a different conclusion. I decided that they were each wrong about the other. The fact is, James wanted sex too, perhaps as much as his wife.

On the other hand, she was hardly "oversexed." Actually, I discovered that she was a much more spiritually minded person than either of them had acknowledged.

What was actually happening with James and Darlene was this: He was trying to be mature and holy by not being sexual. His fight was not with Darlene; it was with his own sexual desire. He had become what Patrick Carnes and Joseph M. Moriarity call a "sexual anorexic."

Carnes and Moriarity define sexual anorexia as sexual self-hatred.[1] A person in the grip of this disorder actually longs for sexual connection but convinces herself that the longing is for something else, perhaps for something spiritual or emotional. Her sexual desire is alive, but she doesn't recognize it or acknowledge it as sexual desire. She will think of it as something else, often as anger. Sexual anorexics often pour their passion into great causes. They are famous for joining great moral crusades against vice. However, the fuel for their crusade is not so much a desire for the common good as it is a need to eliminate the cause of their personal frustration.

Once, when I was explaining this concept to James, he asked me, "What's the difference between a genuinely low sex drive (which is what he claimed was his issue) and sexual anorexia?"

"Well," I answered, "if an asexual person (someone without sexual desire) or a person with a low sexual desire walks into a room of naked people, either of them might ask, 'Aren't you people cold?' A sexual anorexic, however, will probably go into a rage and throw things. Or in your case, he may go pray for several hours.

"A sexual anorexic suffers from a general frustration with life. He or she usually doesn't even understand what the frustration is about. However, the energy manifests itself in other ways. Sometimes it surfaces through arguments about silly things. For some people it arises in spontaneous fantasies and dreams that feel like a struggle against demonic forces."

James looked uncomfortable. I knew that was how he viewed his struggle. I also knew he used pastoral work as a way of running from sexual desire. Only when the desire overwhelmed him would he reluctantly run to his wife for relief. Afterward, he would run to repent.

He was right to feel ashamed. He had never really made love to Darlene. He had merely used her when he couldn't resist anymore. She had often tried to make herself more sexually desirable to him, thinking that was the issue, but as she became more seductive, so did his struggle to resist. He actually had come to think of her as a temptress and a spiritual snare.

She was also right to feel angry with him. At some level, she understood that his prayer was about running from her. Naturally, that felt insulting and humiliating. She was even justified in being angry with herself. Her codependence and lack of confirmation had allowed his crazy behavior to go on as long as it had.

They were a piece of work, this outstanding pastor and his wife!

DEPRIVATION AND SINS OF OMISSION

Christians have traditionally categorized sins as either acts of commission or acts of omission. In other words, we sin either by doing harmful things or by failing to do helpful things. Thus, a man who burns down his neighbor's house obviously sins against that neighbor. However, even if he doesn't actually set the fire but merely fails to tell the person that her house is burning, he also sins against her.

The second scenario, in which a person withholds information that could have saved the house, is an example of a sin of omission. It is a withholding of good that would have brought blessing and health.

Of course, sometimes a person isn't able to give what his neighbor needs. The withholding is still an omission but not a deliberate one. In sociology, we use the word "deprivation" to describe that kind of withholding.

Poverty is an example of deprivation. Children raised in poverty may not receive many of the things they need in order to grow healthy lives.

Emotional deprivation is another example. In that case, a parent withholds affection and touch from his children. It's difficult to know when parents are withholding affection on purpose though. In some cases, it simply doesn't occur to them that they should. In either case, the loss is real, and it damages the children.

Withholding information about life and adulthood is another form of deprivation. Deprivation is at work when parents don't teach their children about sexual things. For example, when parents suppress and shame their children's emerging sexuality by becoming awkwardly silent as their boys and girls experience puberty or by withholding their affection, they deprive those children of the vital instruction they need to navigate life.

Deprivation is as powerful a weapon against life and joy as any trauma or abuse. It is a serious sin of omission against children.

Children can learn how to become adults only by observing how their parents and other significant adults in their lives behave. Unfortunately, if those adults never actually mature, the children cannot develop a clear picture of what adulthood entails. In some families, generations of immature adults have become parents and raised children. In such families, adulthood becomes a foreign and mysterious concept.

In a family without sexually mature adults, the children get the message that sex just comes naturally. There is no need to talk about it because sex will just happen as it should at the right time. This attitude about sexuality is often accompanied by an absence of emotional care. Family members don't touch one another, comfort one another, or encourage one another. There is only silence.

Such emotional and sexual deprivation is a subtle but destructive force.

Most people realize now that if parents don't feed their children properly, those children will suffer the various effects of malnutrition. What may not be so obvious is this: When parents fail to give their children affirmation, encouragement, and instruction, those children usually end up suffering emotionally and socially. This stunting of a person's emotional growth often does not become apparent until she gets thrust into some sort of intimate setting that requires adult skills.

Nearly everyone experiences some early childhood deprivation regarding his or her sexuality. That was certainly true of Pastor James Harrison.

Despite his superficial projection of maturity from the stage, James had unwittingly lived much of his adult life trying to obey his family of origin's unwritten rule: Never grow up.

As therapy continued, James recalled how his father and mother had played with him when he was a little boy. He also recalled that this had all changed when he entered puberty. About the time he turned 13, his parents became distant and cold. They stopped hugging him—permanently. They never acknowledged the gentle teasing of their friends and neighbors about cute girls. They never seemed to notice that James' body was changing. He felt as if a thick silence suddenly descended on his home and that it could only be broken only by the most trivial and superficial of topics.

How could anyone have known that James' personality was beginning to reorganize itself around a core of deep shame?

At James' church, another dynamic was powerfully impacting his young life. He first noticed it one night at prayer meeting after he had given a short testimony about his desire to follow Christ. After that service, a few of the older people warmly embraced him. They expressed their appreciation for what he had said. A couple of them even speculated that he would probably become a pastor, an idea that he soon began to experience as a call from God.

Meanwhile, at school, James felt alienated and aloof from the other students. They talked about subjects that made him uncomfortable and teased him for his apparent lack of interest in girls. They didn't realize he was very interested in girls; he just didn't want to be. For him, sexual feelings were already connected to a sense of shame and defilement.

Masturbating or even having a wet dream drove him to intense prayer. Some of the prayer sessions resulted in spiritual experiences that he found extremely rewarding. They also helped him go for many weeks without consciously experiencing sexual desire. He felt pure and connected to God during such times. Inevitably though, he would have a brief encounter with a girl at school, or he would be exposed to some other sexually stimulating event. Then he would find the urge to masturbate nearly irresistible.

He had no one to talk to about this secret life, which he experienced as unique, isolating, and deeply shameful.

His only antidote for the shame at home and at school was his call to ministry. So he studied and prepared, encouraged by the adults in his life who saw him as a "mature and godly young man." Their praise helped him to ignore his lack of ties to his own generation and gave him a way to escape his shameful desire for sex.

Despite the shame, James told himself that he was on a much higher level than his peers. He found their interests in cars, girls, and sex immature and unspiritual. He wanted no part of it.

Once he was in seminary, he found others who shared his interests. But even there many of his peers seemed unspiritual and unfocused.

He met Darlene in the first semester of seminary. He was quickly smitten by her vitality and creative spirit. She was affectionate but always appropriate. Most importantly for him, she encouraged his dreams about leading a great church. Shortly after graduation, they were married.

James and Darlene were both delighted when they joined the staff of a small congregation in the Midwest. James plunged himself into his ministerial duties. The senior pastor often praised him publicly for his diligent work. The congregation also grew to love him. Unfortunately though, his married life soon began to sour.

After just a few months, Darlene began to feel abandoned and unloved. At first, James listened to her complaints with as much patience as he could. However, he came to think of his wife as lacking the dedication required to lead a great church. He would do it alone, with God's help. Other great men of God had done it; he would too.

He dismissed Darlene's suggestion that they seek professional help. He viewed the idea as both dangerous to his career and unnecessary for a real man of God, so she stopped making the suggestion. She settled into her polite depression that would last for years. She might have continued her education and pursued a life for herself, but the children required care. Also, James wanted her to be a stay-at-home mom. So she read romance novels and watched TV, slowly withdrawing into her private world of silent anger. She began to agree with James' assessment: She was just not a very spiritual person.

James had resumed his old pattern of withholding sex from himself for long periods shortly after their honeymoon. Naturally, he was making the same decision for his wife. Meanwhile, he was becoming increasingly fervent in his prayer and study. His effectiveness in the pulpit made his preaching compelling, and people showered him with praise. As his approval ratings were rising in the church, they were plummeting at home. Naturally, that encouraged him to spend even more time away from his wife.

Darlene had no idea why the congregation's compliments about her husband's preaching made her angry. When she occasionally overheard people say that she seemed unsupportive of her husband, she silently agreed with them. She had no idea why she had become the way she was. She thought of herself as a liability and a drag on her husband's career even though she tried to raise their children and force herself to fit into his world.

When they first came to see me, they had been married nearly 20 years. They had pastored their own church for 15 of those years. As I remarked earlier, I first experienced James as kind, articulate, and focused. Darlene I experienced as withdrawn, depressed, and disconnected.

My opinions about both of them soon changed.

When I asked about their sexual life in the routine intake examination, I noticed both his hesitancy and her interest. He wanted to avoid the subject and gently encouraged me to stay focused on her depression. However, I saw that she was subtly prodding me to keep going.

So I did a genogram—an outline of their families' emotional and sexual histories.

A FAMILY PROFILE

I discovered that James and his two younger sisters grew up in the Midwest. Their father had moved there to find employment shortly after he had married their mother. However, both parents had been born and raised in the same rural, eastern Tennessee community that their ancestors settled in shortly before the American Revolution. Their living conditions back in East Tennessee had been primitive, similar to what one might encounter now in a third-world country.

James' maternal grandfather had been an alcoholic. He controlled his family through manipulation, bodily harm, and insults. James' mother never really detached from her family of origin to form a new family with his father. Indeed, she often seemed bewildered that she had children of her own or about what to do with them. While her children were growing up, she spent her time trying to fix the various trials and traumas of her family of origin. Even after she had moved away, she had focused most of her attention on the mail and the phone, preoccupied with matters back in Tennessee.

James' father was nearly incapable of giving loving touch or affectionate affirmation to his children. He kept family conversation limited to topics that required little reflection and that evoked little emotion. James' sisters remember their father as having a pronounced aversion to sexual situations. On a couple of occasions, as they were visiting relatives in the mountains, he became abusive and cruel to animals he saw copulating in the field behind the grandparent's home.

James and his sisters recall that a hostile silence descended on any mention of sex or romance. The parents did not speak about sexual matters to their children, and the children did not mention the subject to one another. Nor were any of them prepared for puberty. The onset of menstruation pushed both sisters into their own private hell. In retrospect, the family's censorship of sex and adult life was stifling and oppressive. At the time though, they thought of it as normal.

The family's emotional life was carefully regulated. The mother would occasionally get angry and shout, and the father manipulated his family with shaming comments and by giving them the silent treatment. The children never recall hearing compliments, seeing any demonstration of affection pass between the parents, being touched, or being consoled. Emotional nurture was nearly completely absent in the Harrison household.

Religion was the family's one emotional outlet. Three years before James was born, his parents had converted to a group that practiced a strict approach to everyday life but encouraged an emotional response to worship. Their tiny church became the family's only real community. They viewed all other social connections with suspicion and caution.

Given this family background, it is remarkable that all of the Harrison children attended college, married, and showed early promise of living normal lives. Before long, however, the weight of adult life and responsibility began to crash through the woefully inadequate foundation their family of origin had built for them.

As we discovered later, sex generated high levels of anxiety and anger for all the Harrison children. They became mystified, frightened, and hostile at the most basic expressions of adult sexuality. This was true not only of overt sexual behaviors but even of kissing, hugging, and other romantic expressions. In fact, the romantic intimacy surrounding sex was even more difficult for them than its purely physical aspects.

Like James, his sisters married fundamentalist Christians. None of them believed in divorce. Their marriages, though burdened with enormous pain, survived. Meanwhile, the deadly censorship imposed on them by their family of origin continued its destructive work. They each suffered in loyal silence.

Obviously, in a family system that so carefully controls information, learning how to experience intimacy and sexuality is extremely difficult. In the words of Daniel Araoz, "To function well sexually, the individual must be able to abandon himself to the erotic experience. He must be able to temporarily give up control and some degree of contact with the environment."[2]

The members of this family could not abandon themselves to the erotic experience. Letting go in order to connect deeply with another person terrified them.

When Darlene finally insisted that either they were going to therapy or she was calling it quits, neither of them realized how their decision would change the extended family. However, as James and Darlene begin to examine their sexual impoverishment, they cautiously began to approach other members of the extended family. They soon discovered that though not everyone was in agreement about the causes and reasons for the family's difficulties, they were all ready for change.

Slowly, the structure of sexual anorexia gave way, first to overt anger and then to a commitment to find healing and normalcy.

This, of course, is the attitude that makes effective therapy possible. When people begin to imagine they can be different than they are, they inevitably discover ways to empower their hope for change.

For the first time, the Harrisons began to break their family law of silence. They spoke frankly to one another about the early deprivation they had experienced. The Harrisons went from a lifetime of silence about their past and sexual present to an energetic sharing of information, self-exposure, and compassion for one another. Their long detachment gave way to a remarkable determination to find health and joy for themselves and to a commitment to keep from passing to their children the structures of silence and shame that had debilitated their lives.

THE INTERNAL WORLD OF A SEXUAL ANOREXIC

According to Carnes, sexual anorexia is a mental program that contains five core beliefs.

1. Anything erotic is threatening (as opposed to simply human or arousing).

2. Any sexual issue is immediately suspect.

3. Anyone who is sexual is by definition out of control, immoral, and base.

4. Any sexual overture or initiation is exploitive or self-serving (as opposed to loving or intimate).

5. Any sexual desire on my partner's part must be balanced by a greater reserve on my part.[3]

The Harrison family belief system had all five of these characteristics, and they used them to control not only sex but also much of life. It effectively shamed recreation of any sort. Harrisons often started sentences with "I should." Every few moments in a conversation, someone would shame themselves for not attending to physical labor.

The shaming phrase acknowledges what they feel ought to be happening instead of what is actually happening. "I should be cleaning," one of them would say while talking to the other. Or "I don't have time to read this," while reading a magazine. Or "I should be doing my grocery shopping," when watching their children swinging at the playground. In the Harrison family, recreation and self-care were against the rules and slightly naughty.

Karen Horney explains how this inner control, which she calls "the shoulds," works: "The shoulds aim in fact, like any political tyranny, at the extinction of individuality.... They require an unquestioning obedience that is not even felt as obedience."[4]

What Horney describes in that quote is essentially a highjacking of one's emerging self. People who practice "obedience that is not even felt as obedience" replace their own initiative and choice with past generations' anxieties. This destroys a zest for life and creates hostility toward the sources of emotional life.

Patrick Carnes describes the effects of such a process:

> For sexual anorexics, self-hatred often expresses itself as anger. And there is a lot to be angry about. The sexual anorexic is angry at pressure to be sexual by the partner. The anorexic is angry at a culture that seems to create sexual pressures by inserting sex into every part of life. Movies, television, schools, magazines, sales ads, drugstores, and newsstands— all become sources of resentment.[5]

The sexual anorexic becomes increasingly detached from life and grows hostile to those who are not. He suppresses his own desires and shuts them out from his conscious awareness. Each time he fails to recognize and acknowledge his desire, he loses another part of his original self. Life can become so empty that he can finally disappear altogether.

Horney warns, "We cannot suppress or eliminate essential parts of ourselves without being estranged from ourselves...The person loses interest in life because it is not he who lives it."[6]

Loved ones and friends often give up trying to have a relationship with one who is so continually detached. The detached person, so out of touch with her own needs and desires, cannot accept the possibility that her loved one's needs for sexual expression or intimacy could possibly be normal and healthy. The anorexic labels her friends and loved ones as "irresponsible," "hopeless romantics," and so forth. The loved ones finally get the message and give up hope for a relationship.

Carnes tells us why the sexually detached person is confused by her partner's anger.

> The problem of sexual anorexia begins with denial. "There is no problem!" they maintain. Like the food anorexic that denies any feelings of hunger, the sexual anorexic denies sexual thoughts or feelings even in the midst of sexual activity. The anorexic is certain no therapy or help is required. He or she will tend to blame the partner for the frustrations surrounding the sexual relationship. The anorexic may view the partner as undisciplined, impulsive, and somewhat immature.[7]

Even when the detached person enters therapy—which almost always happens when her partner threatens to leave the relationship—she may find it difficult to cooperate in the process of healing. After all, every habit of thought the sexual anorexic has so carefully cultivated battles against the intimacy and disclosure that is involved in effective counseling.

The food anorexic will often begin to label food in strange ways. If she can make food appear demonic or repulsive to her, it becomes easier to avoid. Thus, in the anorexic's private vocabulary, cheese becomes "congealed sweat of an animal's mammary gland," beans become "gas pills," and so forth. A sexual anorexic similarly learns to label her own emotional, romantic, or sexual desires in uncomplimentary ways. The private vocabulary helps her cope with the anxiety that her own desires provoke.

When a sexual anorexic detects the same desires in her loved ones, she quickly moves to extinguish them. She acts as a burn victim might rush to throw water on a perfectly safe campfire simply because her children are standing close to it. Thus, sexual anorexia tends to get passed from generation to generation until someone decides to confront and overcome it.

That is what James and Darlene did. James courageously faced the fact that his sexual attitudes had nothing to do with holiness and everything to do with fear and bad information. Darlene flowered as she realized that James' avoidance of sex and intimacy had nothing to do with her.

Today, they pastor a truly great church that is making a difference in the lives of hundreds. His sermons are informative and seem filled with life and joy. As for Darlene, she teaches a course for mature woman making vocational choices that has drawn national attention. They are grateful for life and relationship, and it shows!

DOCTRINES OF DEMONS: THE EVIL OF SEXUAL ANOREXIA

To most people, sexual anorexia may seem like an impoverishment of life. It is more than that. It is truly a great evil. I was never as convinced of that as when I first read the government's investigation of the 9/11 attacks in New York.

What was Mohammed Atta feeling in the moments before he rammed his 757 into the World Trade Center? Having lived my life around religious people, I imagine him in a dreamlike trance, comforted that Allah was calling him home. Soon, he would be victorious over his sinful nature. He may have been thinking that he, like Samson, was about to strike one of the world's great sources of corruption. Death was a small price to pay for such a victory and for such personal peace.

Mohammed Atta could not have reached this nihilistic moment all at once. He must have arrived through a series of steps, and I would like to know what those steps were.

We can only speculate about Mohammed Atta's inner life. However, our speculation can be more than wild guessing. We have enough information to paint part of the picture.

We know that he was vigilant about avoiding moral defilement, that his family had become concerned with his refusal to date women, that he would not shake a woman's hand. From his will we learned that he wanted his body prepared for burial by "good Muslims" who were instructed to wear gloves so they wouldn't inadvertently touch his genitals. We know that women were not to approach his corpse.

Obviously, Mohammed Atta was in the grip of a serious obsession. At some point he must have decided that he could please God only by going to war against his own sexuality. So it seems plausible that he turned his disgust for himself toward others who, it seemed to him, flaunted *their* sexuality—people like those living in the wicked West, women who tempt and taunt good and righteous men and all other haters of God and holy living.

Atta became, by all accounts, a calm, gentle, and courteous man. However, we know now that this calm was like an apparently smooth ocean that conceals a swelling tsunami. Mohammed Atta's inner storm finally broke through his armored surface the moment he thrust his jet deep into the insides of New York's tallest building. As it spewed out thousands of gallons of jet fuel, he lost his tortured consciousness in the consuming, fiery rapture of death.

For once, a Freudian interpretation seems rational, reasonable, and even inevitable. This was a sexual act by a sexually repressed man. He finally could not hide from the world what he had been so carefully hiding from himself.

This is not just an Islamic problem. Christians too can become so fearful of life that they fail to live it. When this happens in the name of Christ, it subverts all He came to do. Jesus said, "The thief does not come except to steal, and to kill, and to destroy. I have come that they may have life, and that they may have it more abundantly."

When St. Paul calls a preoccupation with sexual avoidance one of the "doctrines of demons," he is only saying what the rest of the Bible, as well as what experience, teaches us.[8] He shows the futility of this kind of thinking:

> If you died with Christ from the basic principles of the world, why, as though living in the world, do you subject yourselves to regulations—"Do not touch, do not taste, do not handle"...? These things indeed have an appearance of wisdom in self-imposed religion, false humility, and neglect of the body, but are of no value against the indulgence of the flesh.[9]

Thirteen

DISORDERED DESIRE

THE NATURE OF PERVERSION AND INORDINATE DESIRE

Malcolm Radisson was out of control. He could not stop drinking, he had picked up a venereal disease from prostitutes, and he was experiencing unpredictable fits of anger. He was in therapy because his brothers had insisted that he get help in order to remain in his management position in the family business.

He had tried AA. In fact, his knowledge of recovery principles was exemplary. He had obviously spent a lot of time reading and thinking about his personal issues. He was an intelligent man whose speech revealed the excellent education he had received from a highly respected university.

His therapist, a bit awestruck at his intelligence, nearly failed to take Malcolm's sexual history. Unfortunately, therapists often overlook this valuable information. When they deal with a person as polished as Malcolm Radisson, they can be too intimidated to ask for such intimate details. However, few things reveal as much about a person as his sexual life.

Finally, Mr. Radisson's therapist did manage to ask a few questions about Malcolm's sexual life. The issue arose naturally as they were discussing the reasons he had decided to enter therapy.

One of the accountants for the family business had discovered what he first thought were minor irregularities in Malcolm's expenditures. He had traced those expenditures to businesses that seemed legally suspect and found out that they were fronts for prostitution. He reported this information to Malcolm's brother.

His brother soon determined that Malcolm had done nothing illegal. The expenditures, though paid to businesses that were legally suspect, were for legitimate business expenses: food, lodging, and such. Nonetheless, the connection with prostitution aroused the family's suspicion, and they discovered the seriousness of Malcolm's sexual addiction.

The therapist discovered that Malcolm had been visiting prostitutes for many years. He had been married twice, but each marriage had ended in divorce before the first anniversary. He also found out that Malcolm was a poster child for promiscuity and sexually risky behavior.

"What is your first significant sexual memory?" the therapist asked.

Malcolm laughed. "That's easy! Mrs. Elizabeth Williams, my eighth-grade English teacher."

"What happened?" the therapist asked.

"She noticed me, that's what happened!" Malcolm replied. "I was always getting passed around from servants to camps, coaches, and what have you. Here was a person who didn't care about my family. She was kind and considerate, and she thought I was smart. Naturally, I worked hard to memorize the poetry, write the essays—all that stuff that kids have to do in an English class.

"She started meeting with me after school to help me with my reading. A few times, she even drove me home. That was before that kind of thing was off-limits for teachers.

"Anyway, about halfway through the year, I found out that my parents were going to California for three weeks, and I told her. She offered to ask my parents to let me stay with her and her husband.

When I agreed, she called and talked to my mother. Mom and Dad agreed to let me stay with her. What my parents didn't know was that Mrs. Williams' husband was also going to be out of town for two of those weeks.

"Her husband was hardly at home, even the first week. Then he left for some place up in Canada. That's when it all happened."

"What happened?" the therapist asked

"She started asking me if I knew about the facts of life yet. She talked about men and women and sex, love and the great romances of history, that sort of thing. We had already talked about this from Shakespeare—the old rascal! What a profligate he was. Anyway, when Mrs. Williams talked like that I just laughed. I acted as if I knew everything already. Of course, I didn't know much. The Friday night after her husband was gone, she came into my bedroom and sat on the edge of my bed. We talked for a long time about this and that. At some point, she put her hands under the covers and started rubbing my leg as she talked, and then her hand went higher. She brought me to orgasm later that night with her hand and then slept the rest of the night with me.

"The next morning, she asked me to shower with her. That's the first time I had seen a naked woman in my life. Then she taught me how to have sex."

"What were you thinking and feeling?" the therapist asked.

"What do you think? You're a man! I thought I had hit the jackpot. I was elated. All those guys at school—particularly the athletes—they were always talking in the locker rooms about what they were doing with girls. I thought about them that weekend. What they had been talking about was nothing. I was getting the real thing."

"How long did this last?" the therapist asked.

"Mostly just those two weeks," Malcolm replied. "We did some things in a car a few times after that—nothing much."

"So you were molested?" the therapist asked.

"Molested? Are you serious?" Malcolm asked. "I was hardly resisting. I thought it was great! I had become a man!"

"If Mrs. Williams had been a man and you a young girl, would that have been molestation?"

"Probably…well, no, not probably. It would have been. Boys are different though. I'm telling you, it wasn't traumatic for me like it would have been for a girl. I loved every minute of it."

Malcolm was getting a bit irritated at his therapist by now.

"What happened to the teacher?" the therapist inquired.

"She moved at the end of the year. I wrote her once, but she never answered. I lost track of her, but I found out a few years later that she died," Malcolm replied.

As the sessions continued, the therapist found out that Malcolm had had sex with hundreds of women after his stay with his English teacher. However, he had never had an actual relationship with any of them. Despite his great promise, moderate wealth, and good education, Malcolm had lived a sad and lonely life.

Mrs. Williams molested Malcolm. He took a long time to own up to that reality; people of his generation usually have a difficult time labeling what he experienced as trauma. However, Malcolm gradually came to understand that he had been a victim of statutory rape and that as a result, his sexual life had been seriously derailed. After the weekend that forever altered his world, the way he experienced sexual desires and the ways he sought to fulfill them became increasingly twisted and disordered.

It would be fascinating to know why his eighth-grade teacher acted as she did. No one seemed to know much about her. We do know, however, that her sexual drive was disordered. Healthy women do not have sex with young boys. Mrs. Williams' story would probably lead us back to an occurrence in her young life that damaged and disordered her sexuality. It is impossible to know.

Sadly, Malcolm's story didn't turn out well. A couple of years after he entered therapy, his sister called his therapist to tell him that Malcolm was dead. He had been alone at a resort in the Caribbean and had overdosed on some prescription medicine, though whether intentionally or not, we do not know.

Disordered sex can kill, though it usually takes a long time.

Despite stories like the one Malcolm told his therapist, our culture now has a difficult time accepting that one's sexual drive can ever be disordered. The term seems so judgmental and intrusive. However, what else do we call the force that motivated Malcolm's teacher and that finally destroyed his life? It was, to be sure, sexual desire. The question is, why did she direct her desire toward a vulnerable student? Furthermore, why did it affect him as it did? Why didn't he just move on and learn to live a normal life? How do we explain any of these things without a belief that sexuality can become warped?

WHAT DOES "DISORDERED" MEAN, ANYWAY?

The word "disorder" implies the existence of order. And the word "order" implies that someone has established boundaries. Our culture finds this terrifying. If we acknowledge sexual norms, then for life to be meaningful and healthy, we must learn somehow to live life by those norms.

This is what one might expect a Christian pastor to say, of course. But we have seen that moralism based on fear and avoidance is no healthier than promiscuity. Indeed, a moral approach based on shame, fear, and avoidance is itself disordered.

We are stuck with sexuality. We cannot refuse to be sexual beings. We can only fail to learn how to manage our sexuality. When we engage in illicit and predatory behavior or try to deny our sexuality, we contribute to disorder and sexual chaos.

Sex is unavoidable, and it is never trivial. The notion that sexuality is an unavoidable part of life challenges many Christians. The belief that it is never trivial rebukes the modern world. However, if sexuality is unavoidable but can become seriously disordered, then a disordered sexuality is an energy that will seriously damage lives and societies.

Our culture is learning about the damaging effects of nonconsensual sex, but it often denies that sometimes even consensual sex can be demeaning and damaging to the human being. However, some of the more distasteful realities of incest and molestation reveal that it is often difficult to define "consensual."

One of the more shameful secrets that plague some victims of incest is their knowledge that the sex they experienced was arousing. This is not true of most victims, of course, but it is true of many. The fact that the victim was aroused does not diminish the devastation it causes him. In fact, it increases the likelihood that his emotional life will suffer profound damage. That was what happened with Malcolm.

The reason that arousal damages a victim is that it seems to discredit any sense of outrage he might otherwise feel. If his own body has betrayed him, what basis can he have to be angry? All that is left is shame and often a drive to perpetrate the disorder.

That unpleasant fact demonstrates the foolishness of our modern tendency to view illicit sexual behavior as a misdemeanor, something like running a traffic light. It's simply not true. Sex is never casual or trivial. It always deeply influences those who experience it, even if they experience it as pleasurable at the time.

Furthermore, this is true for more than just the obvious kinds of predatory behavior. Disordered sex is any sexual act that diminishes the sense that we, and those with whom we have sex, are made in the image and the likeness of God.

Many people in our society now seem to be saying that sex, as long as it does not bodily injure the people who participate in it, is merely harmless recreation, regardless of who participates in it or in what ways. Christians, as well as most cultures throughout history, view sexuality differently. Sex always affects the participants at a level much deeper than their mere physical selves. If this were not true, why is incest such a devastating blow to a child, and why does the victim of incest carry the consequences of the crime committed against her throughout her life?

At one level, the victim of incest, like the participant of any sexual act, has experienced nothing more than the union of body parts. I shake hands with thousands of people every week, and I suspect they are none the worse for it. What makes our genitals different in this way? Why is it that what our genitals touch affects us so powerfully?

Our culture has a difficult time with that question. For some reason, what we do with genitals affects us at a much deeper level than what we do with the other parts of our bodies. We can't seem to acknowledge this in our times, but that doesn't change the reality we experience.

A man and a woman can "hook up" on a business trip while assuring one another that their fling is not intended to be anything significant. They may promise that they are free to return to their own lives and families. However, the sexual union will alter each of them. They will not return home as exactly the same people who left.

In the movie *Same Time, Next Year,* a man and woman married to other people meet one another on a working vacation. They have sex but decide not to leave their respective spouses. The same thing happens when they meet the following year. This becomes a pattern for them that lasts many years. We never see their partners or children. We are led to conclude that this affair is the life that should have been but that cannot be because of the lovers' unfortunate entanglements—their marriages and families.

A similar theme emerges in *The Bridges of Madison County.* An Italian war bride marries a decent, hardworking farmer. She raises children who seem well-adjusted and healthy. However, she is a cultured woman who misses art, wine, and fine conversation. Instead of introducing culture into her rural farming family, she experiences it with a roaming photographer. They have an affair that forever changes their lives. At her death, her children are staggered by the discovery that their mother had loved a man who was not their father.

As far as I can see, these movies are accurate descriptions of how sexual connections make deep and lasting impacts on the lives of those who experience sex and the lives of their relatives. Indeed, these connections become unavoidable and irrevocable once a relationship turns sexual.

This reality, that sex inevitably impacts and changes a person, is at the core of Christian belief about morality. It is not prudishness. Rather, it is an acknowledgment of the power of sex to transform life. That is what motivates (or what should motivate) Christians to set boundaries around their sexual life.

Christians are often charged with cruelty because we teach sexual abstinence for those who are not married. However, Christians believe that the pain of abstinence—and the pain is often real—is much less than the ultimate pain that comes from mishandling the wellspring of life. We are well aware that our culture no longer believes that sexual life requires boundaries. And of course, we struggle with the boundaries like everyone else. Still, we keep teaching and (as best we can) living by the sexual standards stated in Holy Scripture. We don't do it because we are prudes; we do it because we honor life and the Creator of life.

The book of Proverbs tells us that God allows fools to "eat of the fruit of their own way."[1] It's the picture of a man who has rejected the road signs that announce that the bridge has collapsed ahead. He goes on his way to destruction, ridiculing those who are trying to wave him down. In fact, he pushes down the accelerator, laughing at those who are not enjoying the speed and power of his weekend excursion. He laughs all the way to the abyss.

For a Christian, this is a chilling depiction of Western civilization in the aftermath of its sexual revolution. The loss of family, the spread of AIDS, hundreds of millions of babies destroyed in the womb, gender confusion, and a tendency to sexualize all interpersonal relationships—we view this as the sort of chaos and societal disorder that destroyed Babel and Sodom. We want to resist these trends and, if we can, help other people avoid them.

THE COVENANT REQUIREMENT OF HETEROSEXUALITY

In the Genesis account of creation, God creates the universe by distinguishing things. He makes a difference between light and darkness, heaven and earth, living and nonliving things. Then, as He creates human beings, the text stops to remark that He is making two varieties of human beings to both complement and contrast with one another. We are to understand that though both male and female reflect the image and the likeness of God, they do so in different ways so that neither is complete without the other.

This idea of difference and distinction is theologically important. It explains why Christians reject homosexuality as a legitimate expression of human relationship. I realize that Christians often present their objection to homosexuality as though it were a mere reactionary repugnance to the thought that people of the same gender would give one another sexual pleasure. However, from a Christian standpoint, the problem of homosexuality is not mainly about pleasure; it is about the loss of "otherness" that the prefix "homo" indicates. Homo means "same." "Hetero" implies that a relationship contains an otherness, one that requires a person to stretch beyond more of the same. This, we believe, is what God requires in Holy Matrimony.

From a Christian standpoint, homosexuality is a form of sexual narcissism.

Christians believe that God has so ordered the world that our most intimate relationship in life should cause us to confront otherness. We tend to resist this. What heterosexual man has not thought about how much easier marriage would be if his wife were only more reasonable, more practical, more...well, more like a man! What heterosexual woman has not stormed away from an argument with her husband to find complete understanding from another woman by saying in an exasperated tone a single word—"Men!" Heterosexuals tend to desire the otherness when it comes to genitals but reject the otherness when it comes to the rest of life. The differences between men and women drive them to distraction and then to attraction and then to distraction again. Relating to someone who is different is not always easy.

A relationship between a man and a woman is a dance, and dance requires difference.

From adolescence on, most boys fantasize about women. Breasts, vagina, menstruation—all these are infinitely mysterious, alluring, alarming, dangerous, challenging, intimidating, desirable, and intoxicating things. Of course, if we don't learn how to manage this obsession, it can cause enormous ruin. "Manage" is the operative word, by the way. We certainly don't outgrow sexual fascination; those who claim to have outgrown it usually get involved in some sort of moral train wreck sooner or later.

Yet, even although the physical aspects of femininity continue to mystify, a mature man must move beyond the mere physical distinctions between men and women to embrace and, if possible, comprehend the spiritual aspects of femininity. For spirituality, as well as sexuality, manifests itself differently in male and female. Although this is a fundamental truth of life, few people seem to grasp it. Men and women both hunger for relationships in which the partner learns to appreciate and connect with them as they are. Unfortunately, such relationships are rare. They require a high tolerance for difference and the ability to appreciate and to celebrate that difference.

Women often complain about how the culture tends to define sexuality in ways that seem alien to women. Men, on the other hand, are forever complaining that churches tend to define *spirituality* in ways that are alien to the male experience. Sexual maturity (for both men and women) is about recognizing these gender differences without anger or disdain and learning how to appreciate them.

Men are attracted to women who do not disdain male sexuality. Men can, after all, be easily shamed by a need that even they often experience as demanding and incomprehensible. They long for a partner to help them celebrate their sexual desire and control its potential tyranny. On the other hand, their sexual expectations of their partner can be completely unrealistic, though this is not how the man usually perceives it. Only a wise woman can both celebrate and train her partner's sexuality so that it will nurture rather than strangle the relationship. Of course, all of these things are true as well if the roles are reversed, as they certainly can be. I have consulted with many women who desired a much more sexually intense relationship than their husband. The point here is that people seek relationships in which their difference can be understood and celebrated.

It also takes a mature person to accept any reasonable restraints that his or her partner places upon sexuality. These restraints may involve time and place, frequency, and the sorts of sexual expression that will or will not be acceptable in the relationship. If a person experiences these restraints as arbitrary and shaming, every part of the relationship will feel the resulting loss of trust and intimacy. However, if partners learn to accept each other's limits and desires as expressions of their being, the warmth of the intimate connection created in the sexual bond will radiate throughout all parts of the relationship.

Obviously, when the sexual needs of partners are extremely different, the strain on the relationship can be intense. However, this does not necessarily mean that the relationship is doomed. It only means the partners must commit themselves to continual growth, love, communication, and humility. In such a case, growth may result in enormous shifts of personality and character. Of course, that is what conversion means. Thus, it is the very thing God intends of us in our relationship with Him.

Relationships always transform us; that is why they are protected by promises and agreements.

THE DILEMMA OF HOMOSEXUALITY

The culture is currently wrestling with homosexuality, and like so many topics these days, this one is so intense that finding middle ground is difficult. We need middle ground, however. Psychiatrists, counselors, and pastors know that homosexuals often deal with enormous emotional difficulties. Many homosexuals report that they would change their orientation if they could but that their desire for people of the same sex was not of their deliberate choosing. After hearing that same story many times, one begins to gain a respect for it and feels less compelled to refute it.

However, what does a Bible-centered Christian do with homosexuality? On one hand, the Scriptures clearly condemn the practice; on the other, we have compassion for those who feel trapped by an attraction that they did not choose.

The orthodox answer seems trite and perhaps even cruel to a culture for which sexual fulfillment is the core experience of life. However, it is the only answer we have authority to give—that we are all bent and disordered, for that is what "original sin" means. Human "bentness" is apparent in some part of every human being on this planet. So one person is intelligent but drug addicted, another beautiful but not very bright, and yet another is loving but prone to promiscuity.

The law of God judges all these things as departures from God's norm—as disorders. The grace of God, on the other hand, assures us of God's acceptance despite our disorder because "all have sinned and fall short of the glory of God."[2] This acceptance neither condones our disordered lives nor excuses us from the struggle to amend them. Therefore, Christians do not escape struggle but engage it in the company of accepting people and an accepting God.

Liberal Christians have difficulty with this view, of course. They believe that love should conquer law to such a degree that acceptance will put an end to the struggle. Many of us would find this view compelling were it not for the belief that we are eternal rather than temporal creatures. God's grace, in that light, is a transforming power as well as unmerited favor. Grace accepts us as we are but in order to transform us.

Nonetheless, our society now views our rejection of homosexuality as a cruel cultural habit rooted in ignorance. The homosexual suffers, according to this view, because our traditional values impose guilt on persons with nontraditional sexual orientations. In this view, if we will only change our antiquated views, homosexuals will be free to live their lives with their partners of choice but without the complications of guilt.

With the saints of nearly all times, all places, and all parts of the church, we insist that homosexuality is disordered and damaging to individual and societal life.

SPIRITUAL LESSONS

We draw important spiritual implications from the fact that God has designed us to be in relationship with those who are other. For how much more other can anything be than God? However, if a relationship with God involves a stretching toward otherness (which is what the word "holiness" actually means), why would we seek to secularize worship, making it more of the same? If worship is meant to be an encounter with something wholly other, why would we want our church to feel like a mall, a bank, a concert hall, or a theater? In what way could worship possibly be about tasting of the powers of the world to come if we are always trying to remove its mystery and spookiness? Should worship be "homo"—like us and our present culture—or "hetero"—other than us and our present culture? Do we insist that God be like us in order for us to accept Him? Does He want worship to be other so we will move Godward?

If God indeed became a man in order to relate to us, He has done His part of stretching toward otherness. In worship, perhaps, it is our turn to stretch Godward, to press through the discomfort of feeling out of control and to step into the mystery. Otherwise, we may be indulging our disordered spiritual lives rather than confronting the divine otherness that alone has the power to transform our lives.

Fourteen

WOLVES IN SHEEP'S CLOTHING

WHEN PREACHERS BECOME PREDATORS

When Father Joe's world fell apart, he was 35 years old. He had served at St. Ambrose for five years and had come to love its people. He was thinking about that very thing on that sunny spring day he first violated his vows and began his journey of deceit.

Billy was 13. He had been a prize pupil in Father Joe's catechism class the year before. Since then, he had been coming early for mass to help his pastor prepare for the service. He had even begun to wonder if God might be calling him into Holy Orders.

The boy was unprepared for what happened that morning, and I suppose we should note, so was Father Joe. Billy had helped lay out the vestments—the season called for purple—and was about to leave the room where Father Joe was vesting. Then, as he was about to open the door, Billy turned and bumped into Father Joe, who had turned to pick up a church bulletin from the floor. As they looked at one another in amused surprise, the priest suddenly grabbed Billy's face, kissed him, and pushed his tongue between Billy's lips.

The blood rushed to Billy's face as he stood staring into his pastor's eyes. No words seemed to make themselves available for what had just happened. So Billy did what he had been planning to do before the earthquake had shaken his soul: He ran out the door and into the sanctuary. There he said his prayers, listened to the sermon, and went forward to receive Holy Communion. He had fallen into the trance from which he would not awaken until three years later, when he told this story to his school counselor.

Billy's parents had no idea what had happened. They knew only that their son had begun to act differently. He found new friends, refused to go to church, and lost all interest in school. They didn't know that the week after the incident at church, Father Joe had begged Billy not to tell anyone what had happened. "The church would be hurt," he said, "including your parents. Besides, I didn't mean anything by what I did. I really do think of you like a beloved friend."

Neither Billy nor his family had any way of knowing that in the months to come, Father Joe would act out with three other boys in the parish. He would kiss two of them and touch one of them inappropriately. As the boys would later reveal, the priest had apologized profusely to each of them and had spoken to them just as he had spoken to Billy.

Father Joe knew he was out of control, but he had no idea what to do. So he was deeply relieved when, a year later, his bishop transferred him to the other side of the state. There, at St. Cecelia's, he determined that he would studiously avoid all contact with adolescent boys. He was able to keep his promise for more than a year, so he sincerely believed he had put his bad behavior behind him.

Then one day, as he was preparing for a homily, Father Joe discovered a chat room. Teenage boys were talking about sex, and he joined in. He found himself doing this several nights a week after that for the next two months. This was his final undoing. One of the boys' fathers had been suspicious about his son's long hours on the computer, so he printed out a conversation from the chat room and gave a copy to a detective friend. The detective had a hunch that some of the participants were not really teenagers and was able to uncover Father Joe's identity. When the detective realized that Father Joe lived in a nearby town, he filed a formal complaint.

Billy's school counselor filed her complaint the same month.

Because Father Joe's abuse did not involve grosser forms of sexual misconduct and because of a number of legal technicalities, he never served time. But his church ruled that he was a sex offender and revoked his authority to perform ministerial duties.

Today, Father Joe is 45. He teaches history at a community college in a town 50 miles away from St. Cecilia's. Despite his intelligence and likable manner, he seems only mildly aware of the damage he caused not only to the boys he violated but also to the hundreds of people whose faith he undermined. Though he is a predator who wrecked a number of lives, one cannot escape the feeling that in matters of relationship, romance, and sexuality, Joe McBride is no older than the boys he molested.

A Protestant Christian can't help but assume that a connection exists between the requirement for celibacy in the Roman priesthood and the worldwide epidemic of cases like those involving Father Joe. But the truth is actually much more complicated. Reports of sexual improprieties in the priesthood have always circulated, of course. However, until fairly recently these were relatively few, and the incidents were nearly always heterosexual. They also involved consenting adults.

But the Roman church seems determined to suppress the fact that many of its priests are homosexual and that they are not celibate. This present condition of the Roman church in America is due to four causes. The first is the inhuman, unscriptural, and profoundly foolish requirement that its priests must live celibate lives. The second cause is the sexual naïveté that has permeated the Roman hierarchy. The third cause is the widespread belief of earlier decades of Roman Catholics that the sacrament of ordination would sanctify and deliver men of God from sexual desire. The fourth is the erroneous belief of the Roman hierarchy that their first duty was to protect the church as an institution rather than to care for their parishioners' souls.

Enforced celibacy is so weird a practice that one hardly knows where to begin to denounce it. The Roman church does not attempt to defend it scripturally. No pope ever pronounced it to be a doctrinal matter *ex cathedra,* in which a pope evokes the authority of God to legitimatize church teaching. Roman leaders are fully aware of this and do not try to deny the relatively late origin of the practice.

So what keeps them from changing? What else, if not pride?

I am not anti–Roman Catholic. I know and respect many godly priests and lay people. Though I have some important differences of opinion with them, I do not hesitate to call them my brothers and sisters. Nonetheless, something has gone seriously wrong with the American priesthood and has damaged far too many people, including the priests themselves.

It has to stop.

Having worked with many Roman Catholic priests and lay people, I have seen something that the media and the American public at large may find hard to believe: Many of the bishops who covered up the sexual scandals of their dioceses in the '50s and '60s did so not because they were wicked but because they were unbelievably naive. They were so ill informed and fearful of sexual things that they had no idea what to do when they received reports about priests acting out with teenage boys and girls.

Because of this naïveté, a bishop would often respond to a sexual complaint by sending the offending priest to another town. He would do this because he sincerely believed that the priest would do better somewhere else. He tended to believe that a sexual disorder would go away with prayer. He also believed that suppressing information about the offense would be spiritually healthier for the people of the parish. In the '50s, few bishops understood how damaging a sexually inappropriate act was for a child or a teenager. The less said about it, the better.

Then there was the matter of the priest himself. Often from a devout home where no one discussed sex, a boy might declare his desire to become a priest before he had ever dated a girl. He would begin his religious studies in earnest during teenage years. He would experience sexual desire of course but usually thought of the desire as the devil fighting against his high calling. The day would come when holy hands would rest on his head, hands that represented the holy church of the apostles. On those hands were the hands of the apostles and of Jesus Himself. Through those hands, grace would flow that would give power to the priest to do God's work, including the suppression of sexual desire.

We are not surprised that many priests have not coped well with this irrational and unreasonable burden. What is so amazing is that so many of them *have* coped and have served God and their fellow human beings well despite the madness they have tried to embrace.

Celibacy is an option for Christian ministry. No less a luminary than the apostle Paul affirmed that. It may even be preferable, as Paul seems to claim. However, it cannot be mandatory. Any church that makes it so dooms itself to face the kinds of repercussions that the Roman church has been facing in our times.

As for the fourth issue, the misplaced loyalty of the Roman hierarchy, the attitude that compels its leaders to protect at all costs the church as an institution, even from those it is supposed to serve, is hardly unique to Roman Catholicism. Anyone who has served in any church has seen this tendency at work. But that doesn't make it right. No church property, reputation, or corporate mission is worth jeopardizing one soul.

EVANGELICAL HANKY-PANKY

If sexual impropriety were uniquely a Roman Catholic issue, this book would have been much easier to write. Unfortunately, the Protestant world is also guilty of abuse, suppression, and denial of sexual wrongdoing.

Praise Assembly is a large Charismatic congregation where thousands of people used to go each week to hear Pastor Tim preach and to enjoy the soul-stirring music of its worship leader. The church was featured in many magazines and on television programs. However, a worm was in the apple.

Roberto Rodriquez found the worm one morning in late September. Praise Assembly had just hired him as an assistant to the music director. He had been thinking about the Advent season and had some ideas about the Christmas Eve service. He could still scarcely believe the church had selected him, and he couldn't stop thinking about how wonderful the coming Christmas season would be. He was nearly skipping when he opened the minister of music's door and rushed inside to share his idea. He was directly in front of the desk before he saw the bare-breasted woman sitting on it. That's when he saw the minister of music's head on her lap.

He stood frozen until the voice behind the desk erupted into abusive language. Then Roberto made his hasty retreat.

He paced the parking lot for 15 minutes or so before reentering the church building. There, he made his decision to inform the senior pastor immediately about what he had seen. He walked briskly to his office and told the pastor's secretary that he had to see Pastor Tim right away. He was relieved that instead of making an appointment, she picked up the phone to tell the pastor he was there.

He remembered later how he had walked into the pastor's office, had been offered a cup of coffee, and had sat down in one of the plush green leather chairs that faced the pastor's desk. As he stuttered his way through the story, he was so nervous that he didn't really notice that the pastor was not reacting very dramatically to his news.

Pastor Tim was silent for a while after Roberto had finished telling what had happened. Then Pastor Tim began to speak in the soft, kind voice that was his trademark.

"Roberto, you're a good kid. You have volunteered for all kinds of things here at this church, and the people love you very much. We are a family at Praise Assembly. Like all families, our brothers and sisters are far from perfect—like your family, Roberto, I would imagine. Don't you have some relatives whom you love but who do things that you are not proud of? I know I have some of those!"

Roberto nodded his head, admitting that this was so. He even smiled with Pastor Tim.

"Well, Frank has been our music director for years. God has used him in our church in a powerful way, don't you think, Roberto?"

"Well, sure, I just…"

"And Frank has been under enormous pressure with the added responsibilities of this new worship service and all. I'm not taking up for him, you understand, but that woman—I know her kind!—I have been watching her close in on poor Frank while his guard was down. I have been worried about him, and I should have been paying more attention. So I am somewhat responsible.

"I tell you what I want you to do," Pastor Tim continued. "You go back to work. Do the work the good Lord has called you to do. Meanwhile, I will do what I believe to be right about all of this, as God helps me to know what to do. In the meantime, don't open any doors before you knock!" Pastor Tim smiled broadly as he said this.

Roberto remembers that Pastor Tim laughed gently as he led him to the door of his office. He then squeezed Roberto's shoulder as he left the room. The secretary smiled at him and wished him a good day. Although he felt confused, he also felt secure, wrapped up as he was in the love and forgiveness of God's family at Praise Assembly.

What Roberto didn't know was that nearly half of the staff pastors were involved in moral indiscretions of various kinds. "Counseling sessions" were often sexual trysts, pastors had little financial accountability, and no one on the staff who asked questions about any of this survived. Meanwhile, the noses and nickels kept pouring in. Every Sunday morning, thousands of people raised their hands and praised God as Pastor Frank played his guitar and wept about the grace and love of Jesus. Then they all sat in rapt attention as Pastor Tim delivered his spellbinding messages.

Praise Assembly was a predator's paradise. Once a pastor was in the core leadership group, he could use his corporate credit card almost as he wished. No one would ask him to give any account for how he used his time. He could ask the custodians to work on his personal house or car. And, of course, a pastor must do pastoral counseling, which at Praise Assembly, required no training and was not restricted in any way. In fact, that was where both Pastor Tim and Pastor Frank had started picking up vulnerable women.

The stories didn't surface for years. In fact, to this day, many people who once attended there do not believe their church was once a harem for some of the most respected leaders of their community. However, the counselors of the city are well aware of what happened; they were the ones who picked up the pieces of destroyed lives. The social workers know it; they dealt with the church's hostile children who had guessed all along what was going on but had been rebuked by their parents for not having respect. Other pastors in the city know it because they listened to the stories of the people whom the leaders of Praise Assembly had manipulated and abused.

At the core of this spiritual travesty was one of the nicest men you could ever meet.

Pastor Tim doesn't wear a sign around his neck that says Sexual Predator. He seems genuinely compassionate. He immediately puts most people at ease. He looks into one's eyes as he speaks and naturally cultivates a deep trust in those who hear him. He is, in a word, seductive.

His knowledge of the Scripture is poor, his propensity for passive-aggressive abuse is legendary, and his sexual appetite is prodigious, and yet thousands of people vigorously defended him. Furthermore, Pastor Tim does not view himself as a predator. He realizes that he should not have sex with the women in his flock, but he judges these escapades as minor issues compared to the massive amount of good he has done for the kingdom of God. He will often refer to the enormous stress of leading a great church. He will remark sadly about how people who have never tried to do his work simply cannot understand the nature of the load. Besides, letters and e-mails pour in weekly, telling him what a great job he is doing and how his ministry has changed the lives of thousands.

"I am a broken, fragile instrument in the hands of a gracious God," he says with tears in his eyes.

If I did not know Theresa Pomeroy, I would probably cry with him.

Theresa was 44 when she first went to Pastor Tim's office for counseling. She had been struggling with a sense of hopelessness for a couple of years. She felt better in church, but through the week her anxiety resurfaced.

Pastor Tim had walked over to the table where she was handing out brochures for a women's gathering later in the month. He seemed so kind and thoughtful; so she mentioned that she would appreciate his prayers for her because she had been struggling lately. To her surprise, he suggested that she come in to see him the following week.

At the end of the first session, Pastor Tim suggested that they meet again. On the second one, he offered to see her once more. Slowly, she found the relationship turning into a romantic one. In the fifth meeting, he told her that unfortunately, he had developed feelings for her and didn't know what to do about them. She admitted that she was having the same issues. So they laughed and set up yet another meeting.

Several months later, Theresa found herself in bed with her pastor. However, she actually felt bad for him because he seemed to grieve over his waywardness. In fact, during the six months or so that they saw one another, he constantly talked about his brokenness and lamented about how God could use such a person as himself. She would hold him and reassure him that we are all human and that God understands.

The day he told her that he would not see her again, she was grateful. He assured her that he would never speak to anyone about their relationship because he had no intention of "endangering her precious family." She drove home hurt but knowing that though her pastor had sinned, he had still wanted to do the right thing and had a repentant heart.

She didn't know that several women in the congregation had virtually the same story.

Several factors allowed Pastor Tim to continue his predatory activities at Praise Assembly for many years:

1. He was a powerful communicator.

2. No structure existed inside or outside his church with enough will or power to call him into accountability.

3. The thousands who came each week loved him and would not have backed the other pastors, the board, or any other group if they had attempted to remove him.

4. The people in the congregation were spiritually naive, believing that Pastor Tim was much too spiritual a person to get involved in immoral activity. Besides, leaders and lay people vehemently denied and suppressed rumors to the contrary.

5. People who asked too many questions lost their positions of authority long before they became a problem.

Unfortunately, Praise Assembly's story has been repeated throughout the nation. Many of America's most successful churches are family businesses, built on the charisma and/or business expertise of their founders. In such churches, dissent is called "rebellion," and accountability is called "controlling."

Praise Assembly is not what most people would consider a liberal church. A conservative, moralistic stance does not protect a church or a church organization from predatory activity. In some cases, the leader's passion against homosexuality, adultery, and other immoral behaviors creates a smoke screen that makes his own behavior unthinkable to his followers.

THE CLERGY AND INTIMACY IMPAIRMENT

Brenda Palacios was a 16-year-old pastor's daughter whose parents had sent her to me for therapy. They claimed that she had become rebellious and unruly. She was, as they predicted, difficult and short-tempered. Nonetheless, we started getting somewhere in our third session.

"Everyone thinks my dad is so great," she blurted out. "I mean, he is nice to everyone, but I can't remember having a ten-minute conversation with him unless he was mad and preaching some sermon at me. When he's home, he's always on the phone, at the computer, or reading something. He always preaches about family and love, all that crap, but he's like, so *not* connected to me or to anyone else in our family."

Brenda's complaint is one we often hear from pastors' families. When we tell a pastor how his family views him, however, he will often be dumfounded. In his mind, he is carrying the weight of the world on his shoulders and is delighted to get home, where he can just relax and be himself. Unfortunately, he may not have much of a self to offer when he steps out of his pastoral role.

Pastors often play the role of shepherd for so long that they forget the person they once were before they became shepherds. Even worse, a pastor can cease to grow as the years go by, but he may not realize this because he daily hears appreciative words from grateful people whom he is helping. He may not realize that when he arrives to help people face disaster, trauma, and disappointment, his soothing words are predictable and well-rehearsed. People may be genuinely grateful and sincerely blessed for all of that without ever getting to know the real person who delivers the comfort.

As I once heard a priest say to a Baptist preacher, "The problem with you guys who don't wear vestments is that you never take yours off!"

The priest was talking about the voice inflections, physical mannerisms, and guarded presentation, that many pastors assume. However, what may be entirely appropriate for their day-to-day work becomes a mask and barrier for real intimate moments.

Pastors usually believe they have hundreds of friends, but amazingly, most don't have any. They often don't know the difference between acquaintances, with whom they can share life at a superficial level, and friends, with whom they could share their unedited and unrehearsed self.

The realities of the pastoral profession, however, do not stop pastors from desiring intimacy. That is why so many pastors become inappropriately intimate with a parishioner and why that takes them by surprise in such a forceful way.

The person behind the role and mask eventually rebels and becomes willing to risk all in order to be touched and be heard.

THE CLERGY AND MAGICAL THINKING

"Brother, the good Lord and I can handle anything today. I'm confessing that I'm more than a conqueror! Hallelujah!"

That is how Clifford Reynolds opened his first session with his counselor. He was there because his senior pastor had told him that unless he went to see a professional counselor, he would not have a job. The computer tech at his church had discovered that he had been downloading pornography. The porn was not exceptionally vile by modern standards, but at the least it represented a misuse of church time and equipment. The senior pastor intuitively felt that Clifford might have some deeper problems, which he could explore in the safety and privacy of a counselor's office. It was a kind and generous thing for the senior pastor to do.

Clifford, however, wasn't sure. He quoted Scriptures about the elders in the gate, the power of the tongue, the binding of the strong man, and such. The senior pastor had replied to the effect that though he believed all these Scriptures and the concepts they taught, he still believed that Clifford needed a type of help that he was not equipped to give.

Clifford argued with the senior pastor about the counseling sessions up to the very week they began. The pastor remained firm, however. Clifford could go to counseling and begin a spiritual process of rehabilitation, or he could lose his job.

Finally, Clifford went to the counseling office. It was located in a shopping mall across town from the church. As he entered the office, he looked around nervously to see if he recognized anyone. Then he sat down and read a magazine, waiting for the receptionist to call his name.

Once inside the counselor's room, he sat down in a comfortable chair, flashed a big smile, and greeted Jerry, his appointed counselor.

After some small talk, the counselor got to the point.

"So how do you feel about being here because your job depends on it?" he asked.

That's when Clifford blurted out his pious declaration of faith in the Lord.

"Is there a real man behind that religious rhetoric?" the therapist wanted to know.

The question infuriated Clifford.

"Sir, you are an educated man, and I'm sure you mean well, but I am a man of the Spirit. I look to the Bible for my answers, and Jesus Christ is the One who is going to help me now."

"So was Jesus helping you when you were downloading porn?" Jerry asked.

"Are you even a Christian?" Clifford asked indignantly. "If you're not, I don't intend to sit here and let someone try to direct my life who doesn't even know God."

"Hmm," the counselor grunted as he looked into Clifford's eyes. "You're making judgments about my faith and my competence, but you're the one who is about to lose his job because he has a porn problem. Does that seem strange to you?"

"I admit that I have had some problems," Clifford replied, "but I can overcome them by claiming the promises of God, praying in the Spirit, and being vigilant."

"Well, Clifford," Jerry said seriously, "I facilitate a group here on Tuesdays. Everyone in that group is a church worker of some sort. They have many things in common. For one thing, they are all people of faith. Secondly, they all tried to pray away, work away, and confess away their sexual issues. Thirdly, they are all working to overcome their self-righteous and shame-based denial of life and to come to grips with the fact that they are ordinary people, like everyone else.

"You are the victim of magical thinking, Clifford. I have no doubt that you are a man of faith, a good man in most respects. But you believe God will wave His hand over your difficulties and make them vanish. That will save you from looking at your issues, making things right with those you have hurt, joining the human race, and becoming a part of a community of wounded people walking toward wholeness and health.

"So which will it be—more magical thinking, expecting God to brush your teeth for you, shine your shoes, and comb your hair? Or will you walk through the door that your church has been kind enough and spiritual enough to open for you?"

After a few more sessions, Clifford decided to walk through the door. He joined Jerry's group each Tuesday and was amazed to hear other clergymen admit to having difficulties managing the Internet and social situations connected with the church. He listened for several weeks as they asked for advice for dealing with people to whom they felt attracted, with spouses who were drug addicted, and with children who were estranged.

Then one day, Clifford said to the group, "My name is Clifford, and I have a problem with pornography. I believe that with God's help and with the support of everyone in this room, I can live an overcoming and addiction-free life."

"Hi, Clifford," they all said. "Welcome. You're a good man. We're glad to have you."

Almost all Christians believe in prayer and divine intervention. That is not magical thinking. Magical thinking is a denial of difficulties, a flight from responsibility, and a retreat into clichés and self-righteousness. It is one of the greatest dangers to mental health that a believer can embrace. Magical thinking is especially pernicious because it masquerades as faith and trust in God when it actually uses God's name to avoid reality. It is a way of taking the name of the Lord in vain.

THE CLERGY AND ACCOUNTABILITY

Esther McIntire had been an accountant for ten years when the call came from Faith Community Church. The church administrator asked her to help the congregation develop an estate-planning program. The idea was to allow the members to include the church and its ministries in their wills.

Esther thought that was a good idea. She was a Christian and had thought for some time that far too many church people leave their estates without proper guidance. This allows their hard-earned money to go toward people and causes they would not have endorsed. She was between jobs at the time, so she felt that perhaps this was a gift from God. She would be able to work in a wonderful environment with other believers! That made her excited for weeks, even after she began her new work.

She had been at Faith Community for almost three months when the church administrator asked her for help. The IRS was looking at the pastor's personal returns. He needed documentation for some purchases he had made on the church credit card.

"That shouldn't be too difficult," she assured the administrator. "All we need is to show the purpose for the expenditure, the church policy describing the process that he followed, and the final approval from accounting, management, or whatever procedures that the church has established."

There was an awkward silence. The administrator was choosing his words carefully. "We have always felt that a pastor should be respected and that he should not be made to jump through too many hoops. I mean, many churches—mostly ones that are not doing very well—require so many signatures, committees and so forth...we just haven't done that."

"Okay," Esther replied cautiously, "I understand that different churches have different systems of government. But surely someone, some group, at least the board reviews the expenditures. For example, the pastor surely has a budget that allows him to know how much he can spend in a certain amount of time for what purpose."

The awkward silence grew thicker. "Why don't you just look at what we can do?" the administrator suggested.

Esther found that the pastor spent money pretty much as he pleased, and the documentation for the expenditures was scanty at best. Connecting many of the purchases to church work was difficult. Little by little, she realized that the pastor of Faith Community Church was a law unto himself. He had no policies, no procedures, and no process of accountability to follow. The church blindly trusted one man to do what was right.

It was an invitation to mismanagement and abuse. However, many churches run their affairs the way Faith Community Church does.

Many pastors now lack financial accountably because of a historical shift in church authority. Until a few decades ago, most local churches belonged to denominations or associations that provided oversight for local operations. Bishops, overseers, or superintendents asked questions and dictated guidelines for how things were handled. Local churches that did not belong to denominations believed in a system of church government in which a group of elders (or the congregation itself) required an accounting of its clergy about how things were managed.

As some denominations began to lose their power, many local churches that once belonged to them became independent. The newer independent churches, however, never developed a theology for local church government. They frankly became family businesses that served the financial interests of the founders.

That was the case with Faith Community Church.

Brother Roger, the pastor at Faith Community Church, was a powerful motivator. He had done much good for the small town where the church was located. The people in the town respected and trusted him. For many years, as his church was struggling, he deserved their respect. He lived frugally and worked hard. However, when the church began to grow quickly, it never revised its "seat of the pants" financial procedures. Brother Roger continued to make the decisions as he had through the years. But now he was not dealing with $50 here and there. He was dealing with tens of thousands of dollars at every turn, sums that he lacked the management skills to control.

As so often happens, with the money came trips away from home, where he had unaccountable time and unlimited funds. On one of these trips, he visited his first strip club. He was ashamed, but he told no one. A year later, he visited another one. Then another.

Esther had the misfortune of finding out that the Burning Bush in San Francisco was not a Jewish retreat center.

The people of Faith Community Church still think she was to blame for Brother Roger's exposure. The church split that resulted from that exposure left people raw and bitter, and few of them feel warm toward her.

Few people seem to realize that Esther McIntire was not the one who destroyed Faith Community Church. The church disintegrated because of the naive trust that people placed in a good but an unaccountable man.

Churches need either internal or external accountability. External accountability usually flows from a denomination, which has real power to police the theology, finances, and morals of its local clergy and church officials. Internal accountability is a system of checks and balances within a local church that prohibits any single person from acting without reasonable restraints. Each type of authority has strengths as well as weaknesses. Both can be impediments to vision, progress, and effectiveness. Churches are often tempted to throw off all restraints and trust the guy at the helm.

That is always a mistake. Sooner or later, it destroys the man and the church.

A man of God is a man; a woman of God is a woman. People are fallen creatures. They will fail. When preachers have unrestricted and unaccountable access to money, fame, and power, they often become predators. When they do, people suffer.

Fifteen

NO SUCH THING AS CASUAL SEX

A few years ago, one of the respected elders of our church asked me to see a movie called *Fatal Attraction*. I was surprised. It was an R-rated movie with strong sexual content. However, he told me that it was spiritually important for me to go.

Trish and I went to see it together. For the first few minutes, we asked ourselves why this spiritual man thought we should see such a movie. Then the film turned dark. Titillation turned to horror as a weekend affair turned into something that was not a casual thing at all. Before it was all over, blood, death, and destruction had invaded the peaceful home life of an accidental adulterer.

Some Christians might disagree with the elder's ideas on what is spiritually important. Nonetheless, I believe he did the right thing. Since watching that movie, I have faced some temptations. Perhaps, if I hadn't seen the horror of *Fatal Attraction,* I would have had the good sense to resist them, but I'm not sure. I realize that not every affair ends in murder or the kind of outrageous horror depicted in that movie. However, the movie is right to emphasize that we pay a price every time we cross a sexual boundary. People commit sexual sin in private, but its effects are almost always public.

We might say then that *Fatal Attraction* is based on a true story; it is what always happens.

WHAT IS COVENANT?

Genesis 4 tells the story of two brothers who try to worship God without reference to one another. Cain gets angry because his brother seems to have a better grasp on what spiritual life entails. The Lord tells him to be careful with his attitude. "Sin is crouching at the door of your life," God says. "You better learn how to manage it." However, Cain doesn't pay attention to God. As a result, Cain becomes a fugitive and a vagabond. For the rest of his life, he must live isolated and lonely in the land of Nod, the equivalent of nowhere.

Thus, from the very beginning, the Bible teaches us that we must learn how to manage the forces of our lives within relationships with God and others. The modern idea of the autonomous self simply doesn't work.

That's the message of *Fatal Attraction*.

This is probably the most fundamental difference between the message of the Bible and that of other ancient and modern cultures. Aristotle said, "Know thyself." Jesus said, "Deny thyself." These are not incompatible pieces of advice. I certainly have profited from the insights of ancient philosophers and modern psychologists and social workers. However, according to the Scriptures—and I believe the experiences of life bear this out—you cannot really know yourself without first denying yourself. If you become too self-absorbed, always contemplating your own life and worth, you will inevitably plunge into a hell so deep that no drug or therapy can ever pull you out. But if you appropriately lose yourself—that is, turn away from your own pain and loss—and commit yourself to knowing God, learning His ways, and serving Him and other people in His name, you will find yourself.

Dr. Ralph Earle, one of my mentors in clinical practice, wrote a book about sexual addiction that he called *Lonely All the Time*. He came to believe that people were becoming increasingly sexualized because they were so lonely. However, because their sexual experiences were not helping them form enduring relationships, they were becoming even lonelier, which in turn was driving them to ever more frantic and unusual forms of sexual life. This is a picture of how disordered erotic life works to shatter the soul.

To escape this dark hole of persistent loneliness, we must realize that despite our faults and flaws, we have great worth. That perspective is sometimes difficult to maintain. Modern people's motivation to seek for self-realization probably comes from a deep suspicion that we are mere cosmic dust. That is one reason we have a great need to feel sexually desirable to others. After all, if someone longs for me, I can't really be as worthless as I feel. If I have sex with that person who desires me, however, and I realize that she was really after only my body parts, that she never really longed to know the lonely person behind those body parts, what then? I will likely be plunged into a deeper sense of self-loathing. In fact, with the advent of Internet sex, people can have sexual experiences with other people without even touching them. Each person can lie to the other about what she looks like, how old she is, or even her gender.

All this wallowing in artificial relationships leaves us more lonely, not less.

The biblical answer to this existential loneness is for us to live for a purpose that transcends us. If we live for ourselves, we plunge into ourselves and perish. If we live for others, we escape ourselves and thereby experience life and meaning.

Leon Kass wrote *The Beginning of Wisdom* after he had spent 25 years reading the book of Genesis. As he read, he kept asking, what does God want from us? He concluded that God wants us to live our lives transmitting a covenant to those who will be born after we die. In order to do this, we must accumulate wisdom, wealth, experience, and godly character. A part of this growth involves learning how to manage our own sexuality for our own benefit and for the benefit of those who come after us.

Kass teaches that the worship of eros traps us into a perpetual adolescence and keeps us from finding fulfillment. If we are constantly worried about when and how we are going to get our next sexual fix, we never learn to focus on our real life's work. In *The Beginning of Wisdom,* Kass shows how Abraham, Isaac, and Jacob struggled with accepting eros for what it is—a delightful part of learning how to develop a quality of life for one's self and for his descendents. Eros is meant to encourage covenant. Covenant gradually teaches us how to become adults. Covenant and adulthood allow us to manage our ever-accumulating resources for the spiritual, material, relational, and cultural well-being of our descendents.

Thus, spiritual life contains eros but also seeks to transcend it. The Bible encourages us to acknowledge eros and to move through it so we can experience the other kinds of love. The Greeks called these loves *phileo,* or brotherly love; *storge,* which is love of the familiar; and *agape,* which is covenantal love. In his book *The Four Loves,* C.S. Lewis explores this theme in depth; it should be on any serious reader's short list.

Eros feels good but is not always actually good. That is an important distinction to make because maturity is about knowing what is good and then living accordingly. Sometimes that means indulging eros; sometimes it means refusing eros. We cannot do this if we do not learn to experience life objectively as well as subjectively.

When all is said and done then, those are only two ways we can live our lives: subjectively or objectively. The subjective way of life is about judging everything by the way it makes us feel. That way of life makes eros supremely important. The objective way, however, is about judging everything by a standard we regard as higher than nature, higher than the place from where our feelings come. When we become people of covenant, we learn that we must do what is right even when it does not feel good because we know that we and those who depend on us will feel a lot worse in the long run if we do not. Covenant is about keeping the long view in mind. It therefore accepts eros as a part of life, but it also works to keep it from becoming the center of our lives.

Our religious lives will also be either subjective or objective. Either we will serve God and obey Him because it is the right thing to do for us and for those who follow us or we will serve Him only when we feel like it. If we have a subjective religion, we may enjoy singing and swaying to wonderful music about God because it brings tears to our eyes. However, this erotic enjoyment of religious life does not mean that we are actually ready to become disciples. A disciple studies the Scriptures and gradually applies their teachings to all of life. Of course, making a commitment to learn God's ways is not as immediately arousing as, for example, a powerful music experience. However, the commitment will gradually mold us in a way that eventually makes even our arousing and enjoyable experiences much more meaningful.

Covenant teaches us to control nature rather than allow nature to control us.

CULTIVATED NATURE

Most of us have heard the joke about a preacher who tries to make a connection with an old crotchety farmer and says, "What a beautiful garden you and the Lord have created."

The farmer replies, "Oh yeah? You should have seen it when the Lord had it all to Himself!"

Far from being irreverent, the joke reveals an important truth about human life. Art doesn't just happen; it occurs when raw material becomes informed by human intelligence. Gardens don't just spring into being; creative, intelligent, hard-working people must carefully cultivate and maintain them. Likewise, love that creates human families and societies must transcend eros, or natural love. That requires a purposeful commitment, dutiful intention, and plain, hard work.

A WORD FROM DANNY DEVITO

Once, on a flight from Bangkok, Thailand, I watched a great movie called *Renaissance Man*. Danny DeVito plays the part of a smart-alecky advertising guy who has lost his job. His employment agency finally locates work for him, teaching remedial reading and basic thinking skills to a group of uneducated soldiers. As the days go by, a very cynical DeVito is amazed at their growing interest in Shakespeare. The turning point for DeVito comes when the drill sergeant, who hates his guts, gets in his face and shouts, "The difference between me and you is, I care about what I do! I am training men to survive under combat conditions, and I aim to do this job as good as I can."

DeVito suddenly understands that in fact, he has been just putting in time, getting a paycheck for the hours that he works. If he feels good, he goes to the class; if he doesn't feel good, he goes in late, dresses sloppy, and makes sarcastic remarks. The drill sergeant, on the other hand, believes in the U.S. Army and feels that it is his duty to get up each morning to prepare soldiers to defend their country.

DeVito sees that life, which up till then he has lived aimlessly and without purpose, has suddenly handed him an opportunity to lose himself in a cause higher than himself. This truth transforms not only him but his students as well. He becomes a real teacher. When he does, his soldier-students suddenly can't get enough Shakespeare. Furthermore, to his amazement, his students begin to think of him as a man of worth. He becomes gripped by this new perception himself as he sees himself through the eyes of those students. And that is the way that covenant works. We come to know ourselves as we begin to see our unmasked, unedited, and authentic selves through the eyes of those we love. That's why covenant has to precede eros. We have to choose whom we will dare love at that level before we dare unmask ourselves.

HOLY MATRIMONY

Lilly Coleman asked to meet with me because she wanted to introduce her fiancé, Alfred Champy. They had decided that they wanted me to perform their wedding ceremony, and though that would not take place for several months, they wanted to start planning. I agreed, and we set a date.

When they came into my office, I greeted Lilly first because I already knew her. She quickly introduced her fiancé, who was tall and thin. He was casually but tastefully dressed and seemed at ease with himself. I liked him.

I thought that Lilly and Alfred made a lovely couple. They were in their early thirties, were both marrying for the first time, and were obviously in love with each other.

"We want you to marry us, pastor!" Lilly blurted out, more excited than she usually talks. (She is an accountant at a prestigious firm in our city and is normally rather conservative and understated.)

"Good!" I replied. "I'm always happy to marry two people who are so obviously in love. Are you aware of our church's policy of premarital counseling?"

"Oh, yes," Lilly said. "We've already signed up and are scheduled to begin two weeks from now. We're good to go!"

"How about you, Alfred?" I asked, turning to her fiancé. "Are you good to go?"

"But of course," he replied.

I was watching his body language and listening to the tone of his voice as he spoke. *He really loves and respects Lilly,* I thought to myself. *He also seems really smart.*

"We have known each other for three years," Alfred continued, interrupting my thoughts. "We are both Christians. We both like Thai food, and that's a must—how could I marry anyone who doesn't like Thai food? We want to get married and have a family. What more could a guy want? So yes, I *am* good to go!"

"All right," I said. "Let me begin with a little speech. You're here because you want a Christian wedding. That means that this will not be a secular wedding. You could have asked the justice of the peace to marry you, but you have asked a pastor to do it. So I'm assuming you want a Christian wedding because you believe that in your wedding you will be doing serious business with God."

"What do you mean exactly?" Alfred wanted to know.

"A Christian wedding is not a contract, "I asserted. "It's a covenant. A contract is something we do to protect our interest when we are making some sort of business arrangement. For example, when I have my house treated for bugs, I sign a contract with the company. If they do their job, I have signed a paper that states that I will pay them for that work. If the bugs don't disappear from my house, they have to do the job again, or they must give back my money. If they won't do either, I can take my contract to the law. Then the lawyer or judge will read our contract to see what sort of terms we have agreed to keep. When my business with the bug people is finished, so is our relationship.

"A covenant," I continued, "is different. It is giving one's self to another. It is meant to be a permanent relationship. In fact, in a covenant, we don't evoke the law, as we do in a contract, but rather the presence of God Himself.

"So I don't perform weddings that are meant to be mere photo ops and not spiritual rites. That means I'm not interested in flaming clowns, parachuting dogs, or exploding cakes—you can do all of that sort of thing before or after the weeding. The wedding itself will be a holy moment in which we will transact business with God and with His people on your behalf."

"Gosh, that sounds so serious," Lilly said. "Could you give us an idea about what you do in a wedding?"

"Sure," I said. I then took an old leather-bound book from the shelf next to my desk. "Let me read the instructions and vows for Holy Matrimony from this book. All English-speaking Christians used some variation of this service until a few years ago. In fact, if you see a wedding depicted in any movie made more than 20 years ago, you will probably hear the words I'm going to read.

"First, I'll greet the people. I'll tell them why they have gathered and what is going to happen.

> Dearly beloved: We have come together in the presence of God to witness and bless the joining together of this man and this woman in Holy Matrimony. The bond and covenant of marriage was established by God in creation, and our Lord Jesus Christ adorned this manner of life by His presence and first

miracle at a wedding in Cana of Galilee. It signifies to us the mystery of the union between Christ and His church, and Holy Scripture commends it to be honored among all people.

The union of husband and wife in heart, body, and mind is intended by God for their mutual joy; for the help and comfort given one another in prosperity and adversity; and, when it is God's will, for the procreation of children and their nurture in the knowledge and love of the Lord. Therefore marriage is not to be entered into unadvisedly or lightly, but reverently, deliberately, and in accordance with the purposes for which it was instituted by God.

"Did you really hear those words?" I asked. "God established this covenant in creation long before there was a state of Tennessee or a United States of America. Although we are conducting a service that complies in every way with state and federal laws, this covenant evokes a greater authority than what a state or a nation can give.

"Furthermore, we're asking God to join you in heart, body, and mind for your mutual joy and comfort. Because of the joy and comfort your union will bring to you, we are expecting that if God wills, you'll have children who will also follow God, as you have. That's your business of course, but that's what normally happens in a marriage.

"I'm also asking the people of God to witness and bless this transaction with God that we are making, so I say this to the people:

Into this holy union Lilly Coleman and Alfred Champy now come to be joined. If any of you can show just cause why they may not lawfully be married, speak now; or else forever hold your peace."

"Hmm. That's scary," Lilly said. "I have an uncle who may speak up just to spice things up a bit."

"Well, it may comfort you to know that in thirty years of performing weddings, I've never faced an objection in the ceremony itself. The ceremony mostly formalizes and seals the family's support, but that doesn't make it unimportant. The community has an opportunity to speak because this wedding is not just about you two.

"Then I'll turn back to the two of you as I say these words:

> I require and charge you both, here in the presence of God, that if either of you know any reason why you may not be united in marriage lawfully, and in accordance with God's Word, you do now confess it.

"That's the last chance to get off the train before it leaves the station," I said, laughing. "The preliminaries of the service conclude at this point; now the serious stuff begins. Lilly, I'll turn to you and ask this question:

> Will you have this man to be your husband; to live together in the covenant of marriage? Will you love him, comfort him, honor and keep him, in sickness and in health; and, forsaking all others, be faithful to him as long as you both shall live?"

As I read from the book, Lilly looked at Alfred. When I finished reading, she said softly, "That won't be a problem. I can answer right now. I will."

"I thought so!" I replied. "So that frees me to ask Alfred the same thing:

> Will you have this woman to be your wife; to live together in the covenant of marriage? Will you love her, comfort her, honor and keep her, in sickness and in health; and, forsaking all others, be faithful to her as long as you both shall live?"

"I'm ready to affirm those words too," Alfred said.

"Well, in that case, I'll be able to face the congregation and say this:

> Will all of you witnessing these promises do all in your power to uphold these two persons in their marriage? If so, will you say, 'We will'?

"At this point we'll probably move up to the altar. You are free to add music, poetry—anything that is appropriate to a sacred gathering—between any of the parts of the ceremony. This would be a good place to insert a song, for example. After we have moved to the altar and perhaps a song has concluded, we'll begin the exchange of vows. I'll ask you to take each other's hand and to repeat these words after me:

> In the name of God, I, Lilly (or I, Alfred), take you, Alfred (or Lilly), to be my wife (or husband), to have and to hold from this day forward, for better for worse, for richer for poorer, in sickness and in health, to love and to cherish, until we are parted by death. This is my solemn vow.

"At this point, I'll say a few words about how all covenants have symbols that remind everyone of the promises and commitments the participants have made. In our culture, the symbol of a marriage is usually a ring. I'll hold up the rings before the people and say this:

> Bless, O Lord, these rings, symbols of the vows and covenants that Lilly and Alfred are making here today.

"Then I'll give Lilly's ring to you, Alfred, as I give your ring to her. As each of you slips the ring on the hand of the other, I'll ask you to repeat these words:

> Lilly (or Alfred), I give you this ring as a symbol of my vow, and with all that I am, and all that I have, I honor you.

"Then I'll join your hands and say this to the people:

> Now that Alfred and Lilly have given themselves to each other by these solemn vows, with the joining of hands and the giving and receiving of rings, I pronounce that they are husband and wife, in the name of the Father, the Son and the Holy Spirit. Those whom God has joined together, let no one put asunder.

"After this, you can receive Communion or not, and if you do, you can have the entire congregation participate or not. You can also light a unity candle or do other symbolic acts that you find meaningful. I'm open to weave anything else that you want into this ceremony, but what I have read to you are the core elements of the service. Any questions?"

"Pastor, I am happy with what you have said, but tell me, why is it so important to you to have these specific words and this particular format?" Lilly wanted to know.

"I'm glad you asked," I replied. "This is the ceremony that was handed down to us through the generations of English-speaking Christians. I use it for the same reason that you will probably choose a pen with a large feather for people to sign your guest register. I use it for the same reason that you will probably use candles. We don't usually sign papers with feathers now. We don't need candles for light. We choose these things for special occasions to remember where we come from. That's our way of allowing our ancestors to participate with us in this ceremony because we are perpetuating their legacy.

"When you leave the ceremony, you will go on your honeymoon. I hope you have a blast! I want you to have perfect freedom to express yourselves and to explore the beauty of sexual life. As you do, though, you are expressing the life of those who have passed and those who are not yet here. You are stewards and guardians of a long line of people who have a vested interest in how things turn out. This is not just about you or me or even the ones who will be there to witness the marriage.

"We call this ceremony *Holy* Matrimony because it is holy, set apart, different from everyday life. When you conclude the ceremony, you will be different people than you were when you began the ceremony.

"Now I bless you in the name of the Lord. Follow Him, and He will make your way bright and blessed!"

Sixteen

HELP FOR HUMPTY DUMPTY

HEALING SEXUAL BROKENNESS

A friend of mine who was kind enough to read the manuscript of this book as I was writing it had this to say:

"Dan, it frustrates people who have sexual issues to discover merely how they arrived at where they are. Most people want to know what to do about it. Also, as I read, I became concerned about some of the people you mention in the book. Are you going to tell us what happened to them? How are the boys who were molested by Father Joe doing now, for example? Were the people of Praise Assembly ever able to move on with their lives? Did Pastor Tim get straightened out?"

"But Lee," I protested, "these are fictional stories. I created these characters and their stories based on issues I have experienced through the years."

"Yeah, I know," he said. "Still, I want to know who Samantha and Bert are in real life!"

"I can't reveal any more details about Samantha and Bert," I replied. "Their story is just too close to home! The others really are composites and fabrications."

In reality, all the stories are too close to home. I can imagine readers writing to ask me how I knew about their Aunt Rosie. I don't know any Aunt Rosie. I have known many situations that were new to the people involved but were similar to ones faced by people in other times and places. For example, King David got in trouble watching a naked woman taking a bath on a rooftop. The women in my neighborhood don't take baths on rooftops. However, some of them do get naked on the Internet, which indicates that King David's story is shared by thousands.

Nonetheless, my friend is right; when we face sexual issues, we want answers, not just interesting stories.

Another problem one faces when writing a book about sex is how to use humor properly. Sexual difficulties are heartbreaking. Besides, sexual humor is often coarse or degrading. Some would think that sexual humor is rarely if ever appropriate. However, when the subject gets too tense, humor is often the only way to break through the gloom. Besides, humor may be the natural and reasonable response of creatures like ourselves, wedged as we are between animal and angel.

Finally, though, sexual issues are serious. Sexual trauma shatters people as few events in life can. An affair, molestation, or addiction often leaves a person fragmented and seemingly incapable of normalcy. In fact, I have often used the story of Humpty Dumpty to explain the impact of sexual devastation on the human personality. It's a humorous way to talk about tragic situations.

THE INCREDIBLE, BREAKABLE EGG

Even as a child, I didn't believe we had the whole story about what happened up on that wall before Humpty Dumpty had his famous fall! All we know is that a poor guy sat on the wall and that he had a great fall. We don't even know if anyone pushed him. We know that after he fell, all the king's horses and all the king's men couldn't put him together again. (Of course, I have always wondered what anyone expected of the horses to begin with!)

The musical group Counting Crows once sang about how Humpty Dumpty was beyond help, but I don't buy that. (Besides, I don't have much patience with a group that can sing about Albert Einstein and Humpty Dumpty in the same song!) So I have consulted children, the real authorities about Humpty Dumpty.

Most children believe that Humpty Dumpty brought his fall on himself. After all, an egg shouldn't be sitting up on a wall. My response to that is that we're not altogether sure that he was an egg. That idea came from an illustration in a Mother Goose book, and what does she know?

I believe Humpty Dumpty is a picture of our Western culture.

If we listen very long to our mental-health professionals, social workers, and political commentators (on both the right and the left), don't they seem a little like all those king's horses and all those king's men, working furiously to put Humpty Dumpty together again? Doesn't the Western world seem cracked and impossible to fix?

Maybe that's what Counting Crows had in mind when they sang their strange lyrics about a disappearing world, too fragmented now to reassemble itself. (Whether Einstein caused it or not is another subject!)

Whoever caused the damage, for more than a century our culture has been trying to figure out what to do about the broken state of humanity in Western civilization. In the first year of the last century, a young doctor named Sigmund Freud started writing about what he believed about human consciousness. First the city of Vienna and then all of Western civilization began to shudder at the impact of his words.

I became interested in Freud when I began my college work. In a short paper on the history of psychology, I made what I thought was a clever but derogatory remark about him. When I got the paper back, the professor had written in the margin, "Cute remark about Freud. It would have been a lot cuter if you had ever read him."

The remark stung me, so I decided to read some of Freud's major papers. I discovered that he was always intriguing, even when I disagreed with him.

Freud actually restated something the prophet Jeremiah had said thousands of years before: "The heart is deceitful above all things and desperately wicked; who can know it?"[1] Augustine and Shakespeare had also concluded that much of the content of the human mind remains inaccessible even to its owner. Freud, however, stated his ideas in a modern and secular language that claimed to be scientific.

People took note of his work, and it quickly became a new orthodoxy of thought about human mind and intention.

After Freud came hundreds of new theories and dozens of new fields. Mental health, social action, psychopharmacology, and 12-step groups; inner child, transference, denial, and lithium; shock therapy, Zoloft, and ink blots; collective unconsciousness, ego state, and Dr. Phil—we ultimately owe all of this to the strange doctor from Vienna and his studies of "hysteria." For well over a century now, all these king's horses and king's men have been trying to put Humpty Dumpty together again. And yet we remain broken.

This brokenness is especially obvious in our sexual lives, the area to which our culture has given so much of its attention. The culture keeps requiring sex to live up to its promise to give us meaning and a reason to live. Yet this search for sexual nirvana drives us to behaviors that often leave us ashamed and shattered.

It is an old story, from King David to Aunt Rosie and the characters in this book.

Naturally then, my friend wanted to know what the characters in this book had done to get help. He also wanted to know if the help they received had made a difference. Unfortunately, some of the characters in this book did not find healing and transformation. Some did not seek help. Others sought it but would not do the difficult work required to apply the knowledge they received. Yet others sought help too late; they had already allowed their spirits to be crushed under the mountains of guilt, loneliness, and fatigue.

Those who did find healing and transformation experienced it by walking through a few steps available to everyone. We will end this book by talking about those steps.

WAKE UP!

The first step in getting help for sexual dysfunction is simply realizing that something is wrong.

Walter Meadows had his wake-up moment the night his six-year-old daughter nearly walked in on him and a prostitute. For some time, he had been periodically cruising a certain street in our city where he knew he could pick up women. He would pay one and then have her do some sexual act in the car. This time, though, his wife was out of town, so he decided to call one of the women and have her come to his house for the evening. He had put his daughter to bed and thought she was sound asleep when the hooker arrived.

They went into his bedroom, where they began to drink and then to take off their clothes. He was horrified, however, when the door to his room opened. There stood his daughter, holding her teddy and crying about having a bad dream. Fortunately, he was partly covered by a blanket. Also, his visitor was in his bathroom and had enough sense not to come out until the little girl had returned to her room.

He was finished though. He paid the woman and then wept through the night. Deeply shamed, he called me the following morning and begged for help.

His story had a good ending. A few weeks later, he confessed to his wife that he had been living a double life. He entered a serious treatment program and went through a formal confession with his pastor. Many years have passed, and Walter Meadows continues to live in the light. He has had the great joy of watching his daughter grow up loving and respecting him. As for his daughter, she has no idea that she helped save her dad from ruin and death.

Walter's case is rare, unfortunately. Something in him snapped before things had gone too far. He became determined to do whatever was necessary to save himself and his household.

For some people, the wake-up call is a police car, a venereal disease, or divorce papers. Even these traumatic situations can become angels of mercy; recovery groups are filled with people who testify that the worst day of their life became the best day of their life. Waking up from addiction and dysfunction is always difficult; who likes an alarm clock? On the other hand, who wants to spend their life asleep at the wheel?

WORKING THROUGH SHAME

Sexual dysfunction is embarrassing! We get the impression from the media that everyone else has this area of life down pat. The guys down at the gym seem to be doing fine because we hear them talking in the locker room about how good their sex lives are. The magazines at the supermarket checkout are covered with beautiful people who all have wonderful sex. We could easily assume that the main sexual concern of the people around us is about "Finding That Special Spot!" or "Six New Things That Will Drive Him out of His Mind!"

Paying for your groceries, trying not to let the checkout person see where you are looking, you think, *What special spot? That must be what's wrong with our sex life—I haven't found the special spot...I'll get the magazine and leave it laying around so my wife can read about the six new things that will drive me out of my mind...Who discovered these six new things, I wonder? Gee, what could those six new things be? I bet the guys at the gym have girlfriends that read that magazine and they've already been driven out of their minds several times this week. I hope they're all in traction now...No, I don't mean that...Well, yes I do! Anyway, I can't buy that magazine; the checkout girl knows my secretary, she'll tell a few people, and then everyone will know that I don't have a clue about the six new things.*

So what can one possibly do about things such as premature ejaculation, vaginismus, Internet porn addiction, erotic fixation with one's dentist, and all the other obsessions and dysfunctions to which we are prone? *The guys at the gym don't deal with this stuff, after all. The women in the prayer group never wrestled with such stuff! I think I'll just keep quiet,* you think.

Shame and the fear of exposure work in our favor when we want to make jokes about sexual stuff. Men try to employ shame all the time when trying to get the best of a friend. For example, I waited for years until I found the perfect opportunity to get one over my friend John.

I had injured something in my lower back and couldn't move very well. I had been suffering for weeks. John was trying to help me get my work done, so I feel a little guilty about what I did to him (but not much). He had helped me get into a restaurant for lunch and was watching me grimace as I moved into the booth. After we had sat down to eat, he asked me with uncharacteristic sympathy, "Dan, what in the world did you do to your back, anyway?"

That was my cue! I had waited for such an opening.

"Well, John," I replied, "it's sort of embarrassing. I should have just told Trish I had had enough after the third go-round that night."

For a few seconds, he looked positively smitten. Then he spat out a single word: "Liar!"

He was right. I was lying. But that's how guys talk about sexuality. He knew me too well for the lie to convince him—and, I hasten to add, lying is against the Ten Commandments, and I realize that this commandment is always in force, even in situations like this, in which it is soooo tempting. On the other hand, his sympathy and concern opened up an opportunity…again, it wasn't right; I know that. But I had my moment, and it's difficult not to feel proud about it!

Most of the time, shame isn't funny.

Rebecca, who you will remember once got her kicks doing nasty things to her boyfriend while he was driving, thought she would die the first time she went to a Sexaholics Anonymous group.

"I was so humiliated, Dan," she said. "I sat down in the circle and decided just to listen for a while. One guy had gotten fired for exposing himself to a female colleague at work. He told us that because she smiled at him and had laughed at a sexual joke in the lunchroom, he thought she would find his actions arousing. He had asked her to come into his office. Then, he asked her to move around to the other side of his desk so he could show her something. She had no idea that he had opened his pants and exposed his penis.

"'I was shocked,' he said, 'when she filed the complaint. I really expected her to invite me into a closet for sex or something like that.'

"Another man told us how he had spent his life savings on sleazy massage parlors.

"There were tears in that room and so much regret. When it came my turn to talk, I nearly passed out. I sobbed as I told the group how we had endangered people's lives on the highway. When I was finished, they all just welcomed me to their group. Week after week, month after month, I checked in and told them when I was tempted to act out. I told them everything. Sometimes they were a bit rough if they thought I was holding back or justifying my behavior, but they taught me what grace was all about.

"I called them the Shame Busters! Without them, I might have never found my way back to sanity."

When people have acted out sexually, or when they are carrying a secret about sex, they need friends. However, they need people who will neither excuse what is inexcusable nor withdraw from them when the truth comes out. Healing begins when one is able to tell the truth (regardless of how painful it is) and discover that the truth does not alienate real friends. That allows one to remove the false face forever.

ACCOUNTABILITY AND COMMUNITY

Accountability is not police work; it is telling the truth in love. It is asking difficult questions. It is refusing to allow one to hide or dodge. When Trish and I were going through the most intense part of our counseling, my friend John knew I was vulnerable. He became afraid that I would mess up, so he called me every day. Sometimes, he called several times a day.

"Where are you?" he would ask. "What are you doing?"

"Oh, just messing around," I might say.

"Define 'messing around,'" he would demand.

I made it through the storm without royally messing up my life because I had him, a great secretary, a good wife, a number of therapists, and a small recovery group that met each Tuesday morning. All of them asked questions, and all of them expected answers. However, they also all loved me. Their questions were not meant to shame or to control me. They knew I was facing a rough period of my life. They wanted to help me make it through.

My friends Ed and Yvette even gave me a key to their house. Trish was in the hospital for an entire summer, and their house was nearby. "When you just don't feel like going home, Dan, you have a room here. It will be always ready for you. Please don't isolate yourself; you'll get in trouble if you do," they said.

A few times, I did drive to their house and crash at my little room there. It became my safe place. They were safe people. They absorbed my pain and lovingly made sure that I was "walking the walk." Their house became my storm shelter.

Whatever I do that is a blessing to anyone, I owe to those who helped keep me accountable through the stormy years. Only God knows what they saved me from, and I am grateful.

Healing requires community. Sometimes, we go through a season in which we must surrender a measure of our independence in order to survive. The interdependence we cultivate during such times prepares us for the healthy independence we can enjoy later.

An interdependent healing community takes many forms. For me, it consisted of a few leaders at my church, my 12-step group, my therapists (especially Marylyn, Ken, and Dianne), my fellow pastors in the city where I worked and who faithfully met with me once a month, and finally, the good people of the Anglican Mission in America (especially Bishop Alexander Greene), who offered me a place to keep growing in God. And though this is not often the case for others, my wife, children, and sons-in-law also joined my healing network.

When we are addicted or dysfunctional in some other way, we tend to think that we can make things better all by ourselves. We want to get well without dropping our false face. Our constructed personality keeps warning us that no one will love us if we stop hiding our true face. Unfortunately, getting well requires the deconstruction and death of the constructed personality. That scares us. But we are surprised to find out that when we finally get real, when we finally allow our friends to see our real face, they nearly always laugh and say, "So that's what you really look like? Cool!"

A LIFELONG COMMITMENT TO HEALING

Corrie ten Boom tells the story about a Roman Catholic priest in Amsterdam who had been notorious for visiting the red-light district. When the Nazis took over, they rounded up religious leaders and prostitutes and put them in camps. They thought it would be funny to put this particular priest with the prostitutes. However, the priest gathered the ladies together and confessed his sins. He said, "All of Amsterdam knows that I have not lived like a man of God. I do, however, intend to die like one." Before he died, he had baptized dozens of women, taught them about the Lord, and prepared them to meet God. After the war, his story spread. The Christians of Holland honored him in death as a godly man. If nothing else, the fact that I can use his story means that his decision to live a new kind of life did not come too late.

Like that priest, we have to make a decision. Then we have to reveal our stuff to those we have harmed. We have to continue our journey in community with great humility of heart. And we have to keep our eyes on the great prize so that our living will not be in vain. That's how Humpty Dumpty gets put back together again.

I could think of no better way to end this chapter and this book than to refer you to Varn Michael McKay's song, "The Potter." In fact, I suggest you find Walter and Tramaine Hawkins' rendition of the song, get a box of Kleenex, turn up the volume, and prepare to praise God for His irresistible grace.

The song is about the time God directed the prophet Jeremiah to visit a potter's shop. When he got there, he began watching how the craftsman reassembled pieces of broken pottery to make an even more beautiful work of art than before.

Every time I hear that song I think about the time I was serving Communion at a small gathering in a private home. The homily at the service was given by an artist who told the story of how she had crafted a piece of pottery for the church. After she finished it, she discovered it did not meet up to her expectations. In her anger, she slammed it against the wall, where it shattered into pieces. As soon as the pottery hit the wall, she felt shamed by her lack of self-control. She believed God would have her pick up all the pieces and reassemble them.

She took weeks to reassemble the pieces and glue them together. At first, she wondered what she would do with it. Then she decided to offer it as an altar piece.

The worship leader experimented and saw that a votive candle fit perfectly inside the pottery.

After her homily, we prayed for forgiveness for our sins. I said these words: "All who have truly and earnestly repented of your sins, and are in love and charity with your neighbors, and who intend to walk in new life for the glory of God, draw near in faith." As I spoke the words of invitation to the Lord's Table, I watched the flickering flame of the candle glowing from within the reassembled piece of pottery. The light was dancing on the altar, on the chalice, and on the faces of all those close to the Lord's Table.

I thought about how the light would have never danced had it not been for the cracks in the art.

Notes

INTRODUCTION

1. A reference to Hebrews 6:5 (KJV).

2. Peter Kreeft, *Ecumenical Jihad: Ecumenism and the Culture War* (San Francisco: Ignatius, 1996), 16.

3. From the Westminster Confession.

CHAPTER 1—A BIG FAT JEWISH WEDDING: WHY JESUS ATTENDED A WEDDING AND TURNED WATER INTO WINE

1. "For the young men in the taverns or the young women in the vineyard, the Song needed no interpretation, whatever the theologians were saying." Ariel Bloch and Chana Bloch, *Song of Songs* (Berkeley: University of California Press, 1998), 30.

2. The translation of the verses from Song of Solomon in this chapter are from Bloch and Bloch, *Song of Songs.*

3. See Psalm 84:11.

4. See Ephesians 5:18.

5. See Ecclesiastes 3:1.

6. John 2:5

CHAPTER 2—GROW UP! WHY HOLINESS DOES NOT MEAN PREPUBESCENCE

1. Proverbs 4:7

CHAPTER 3—GOOD SEX: WHEN BODY AND SOUL COME TOGETHER

1. 1 Corinthians 6:15-16

2. Hebrews 12:16

3. Mark 10:9

CHAPTER 4—MAY I HAVE YOUR ATTENTION? FOCUSED AWARENESS IN SEX AND SPIRITUAL LIFE

1. Daniel Goleman, *Vital Lies, Simple Truths: The Psychology of Self-Deception* (New York: Simon and Schuster, 1985), 21.

2. 1 Corinthians 13:12

CHAPTER 5—THIS IS MY BODY: THE IMPORTANCE OF INTIMACY

1. Hebrews 10:31

CHAPTER 6—GROANINGS THAT CANNOT BE UTTERED: WHEN INTIMACY GOES BEYOND WORDS

1. Romans 8:26

2. For an accessible summary of Tomkin's work, see Eve Kosofsky Sedgwick and Adam Frank, *Shame and Its Sisters: A Silvan Tomkins Reader* (Durham, NC: Duke University Press, 1995).

3. Sedgwick and Frank, *Shame and Its Sisters,* 58 and following.

4. Hebrews 5:7

5. 1 Corinthians 14:14-19

CHAPTER 7—I'M BESIDE MYSELF!: THE ROLE OF ECSTASY IN SEXUAL AND SPIRITUAL LIFE

1. Psalm 150:4

2. Acts 22:17; 10:10

3. Proverbs 7:17-23

4. Hebrews 11:6

CHAPTER 8—THINK ABOUT IT! THE ROLE OF SEXUAL IMAGINATION

1. Matthew 5:28

CHAPTER 9—TRAINING WHEELS: THE ROLE OF MASTURBATION IN SEXUAL LIFE

1. Quoted in Martha Cornog, *The Big Book of Masturbation: From Angst to Zeal* (San Francisco: Down There Press, 2003), 195.

CHAPTER 10—THE UNKINDLY CUT: WHY CIRCUMCISION?

1. Leon Kass, *The Beginning of Wisdom: Reading Genesis* (Chicago: University of Chicago Press, 2006), 72.

2. Kass, *The Beginning of Wisdom,* 63.

3. Kass, *The Beginning of Wisdom,* 91.

4. Wendy Shalit, *A Return to Modesty: Discovering the Lost Virtue* (Glencoe, IL: Free Press, 2000). Quoted in Daniel R. Heimbach, *True Sexual Morality: Recovering Biblical Standards for a Culture in Crisis* (Wheaton, IL: Crossway, 2004), 199-202.

CHAPTER 11—CAN'T GET ENOUGH: THE BONDAGE OF SEXUAL ADDICTION

1. Ernest Kurtz and Katherine Ketcham, *The Spirituality of Imperfection: Storytelling and the Journey to Wholeness* (New York: Bantam, 1992).

2. Romans 4:17

CHAPTER 12—CAN'T TOUCH THIS:
THE AGONY OF SEXUAL ANOREXIA

1. Patrick Carnes and Joseph M. Moriarity, *Sexual Anorexia: Overcoming Sexual Self-Hatred* (Center City, MN: Hazelden, 1997).

2. Daniel Araoz, *The New Hypnosis in Sex Therapy: Cognitave-Behavioral Methods for Clinicians* (Northvale, NJ: Aronson, 1998), 77.

3. Carnes and Moriarity, *Sexual Anorexia,* 46.

4. Karen Horney, *Neurosis and Human Growth* (New York: Norton, 1950), 118.

5. Carnes and Moriarity, *Sexual Anorexia,* 41.

6. Karen Horney, *Our Inner Conflicts: A Constructive Theory of Neurosis* (New York: Norton, 1945), 111.

7. Carnes and Moriarity, *Sexual Anorexia,* 51.

8. 1 Timothy 4:1-5

9. Colossians 2:20-23

CHAPTER 13—DISORDERED DESIRE:
THE NATURE OF PERVERSION AND INORDINATE DESIRE

1. Proverbs 1:31

2. Romans 3:23

CHAPTER 16—HELP FOR HUMPTY DUMPTY:
HEALING SEXUAL BROKENNESS

1. Jeremiah 17:9

OTHER GREAT
HARVEST HOUSE READING

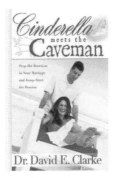

CINDERELLA MEETS THE CAVEMAN
Dr. David E. Clarke

As women continue to live out Cinderella-like roles and men repeat caveman-like behaviors, boredom can drain the spontaneity and joy out of their relationships. With humor and insight, David Clarke empowers you to build intimacy by creating a romantic mood, meeting core needs, and achieving a one-flesh connection.

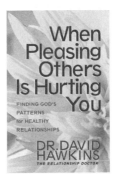

WHEN PLEASING OTHERS IS HURTING YOU
Dr. David Hawkins

When you begin to forfeit your own God-given calling and identity in an unhealthy desire to please others, you move from servanthood to codependency. This helpful guide can get you back on track.

MEN ARE LIKE WAFFLES—
WOMEN ARE LIKE SPAGHETTI
Bill and Pam Farrel

Take a fun look at how God made us and the many different ways men and women regard life, marriage, and relationships.

To learn more about Harvest House books
or to read sample chapters, log on to our website:

www.harvesthousepublishers.com

HARVEST HOUSE PUBLISHERS

EUGENE, OREGON